Books in the How To Play Series

How to Play Bass Guitar
BY LAURENCE CANTY

How to Play Drums
BY JAMES BLADES AND JOHNNY DEAN

How to Play Guitar
BY ROGER EVANS

How to Play Saxophone
BY JOHN ROBERT BROWN

How to Play Keyboards
BY ROGER EVANS

How to Play Piano
BY ROGER EVANS

HOW TO
PLAY THE FLUTE

HOW TO PLAY THE FLUTE

Everything You Need to Know to Play the Flute

Howard Harrison

**Illustrated by
Neil White**

St. Martin's Griffin
New York

HOW TO PLAY THE FLUTE. Copyright © 1982 by EMI Music
Publishing Ltd. All rights reserved. Printed in the United
States of America. For information, address St. Martin's Press,
175 Fifth Avenue, New York, N.Y. 10010.

www.stmartins.com

Library of Congress Cataloging-in-Publication Data

Harrison, Howard.
   How to play the flute.
   ISBN 0-312-28861-1
   1. Flute—Methods—Self-instruction. I. Title.

MT348.H37   1983
788'.51'0712   83-15927

First published in Great Britain by Elm Tree Books Ltd.

20 19 18 17 16 15

Contents

HOW TO
PLAY THE FLUTE

Introduction

Perhaps you have already flipped through this book. You will have noticed plenty of music, of course; a flute tutor wouldn't be much without that. What may have surprised you is the amount of writing and explanation which it also contains, because most flute tutors devote only three or four pages to telling you how to read music and produce a sound from your flute — then they follow that up with yards and yards of music as if there were nothing more to it and that no further explanation were necessary. This is an encouraging impression to give, but, unless you have a good teacher to answer all your queries and explain all those things left unexplained, I know that it is a recipe for frustration.

Now it is certainly true that no book can communicate the beautiful and intriguing business of playing the flute as well as a good teacher, but I felt that it would be valuable if, for once, someone would write a tutor which really did communicate the basics of good flute-playing in an unmysterious but thorough way, anticipating and meeting the beginner's inevitable questions, and not chickening out and saying 'ask your teacher' when the questions got tricky!

If you are teaching yourself, you will find the 'extra' help and advice in this book invaluable. If you are having lessons, then you will find How to Play the Flute a valuable reference, as well as a source of over 50 new pieces to play.

How can I improve my tone? How can I work out how this piece goes? Why won't this note come out as it should? The answers are all here.

Howard Harrison

PART ONE
Basics

The first section of this book shows you how to make your first sound on the flute and contains a lot of important, basic information. Much of this is included partly for reference, so you needn't attempt to memorise any of it. However, do be sure to read it all before you go on to part two.

Your Flute

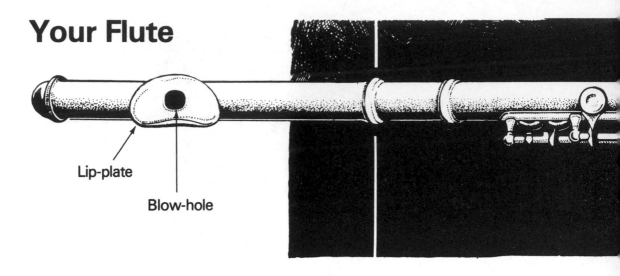

Head joint

Lip-plate

Blow-hole

Your beautiful flute is most likely to be damaged when you are putting it together! Here is how to assemble your flute correctly and without any risk of damage to its mechanism.

First, insert the open end of the head joint into the end of the middle joint which has no keys on it. Grip the middle joint where there are no keys and use a gentle to and fro twisting motion to ease what should be a smooth but air-tight fit.

The centre of the blow-hole should be in line with the centres of most of the keys on the middle joint. On most flutes, there is a system of arrows or lines to help you make this alignment. If your flute doesn't have one, use a straight edge to get the alignment right the first time and, when it *is* right, put a couple of tiny scratches or sticky markers on the underside of the flute, one on the head joint and one on the middle joint, for future reference.

Always fit the head joint in *exactly* the same position.

The foot joint, of course, fits on the other end of the middle joint. The rod to which the keys of the foot joint are attached should be lined up with the centre of the last key on the middle joint. Again, be gentle and avoid handling the mechanism.

If the joints of your flute feel very tight, or if they stick, wipe both of the surfaces which come into contact. Flute joints are made to exact specifications and it is a build-up of dirt and grit rather than a lack of lubrication that makes them stiff. If you should need to grease them, a tiny spot of petroleum jelly (vaseline) will be enough.

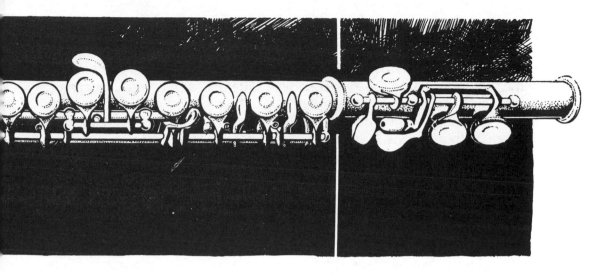

Middle joint

Foot joint

Pin Springs

When a key is pressed and then released, it is one of these springs which returns it to its original position. Occasionally, the free end of a spring might slip out of place. It can be poked back into position with the tip of a tiny screwdriver.

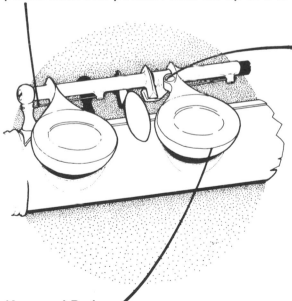

Adjusting Screws

Not all the keys on the flute are pressed with the fingers, but those which aren't are coupled to ones which are. Any linked pair of keys must go down exactly together otherwise one of them won't form a seal. A *small* movement of an adjusting screw will advance or retard the action of a linked key to get the timing right. Don't touch these screws unless you feel quite sure of yourself!

Keys and Pads

Each of the metal keys has a soft pad inside it. When a key is pressed, its pad should form an air-tight seal with the raised rim of the hole underneath. Look out for bent keys and worn pads and have them straightened or replaced.

How the flute makes a sound

The flute that you are learning to play is just one member of an ancient and enormous family of musical instruments. Despite superficial differences, recorders, ocarinas, whistles, fifes and panpipes are all types of flute. These and hundreds of other instruments are related to one another because they all employ the same simple means to produce their sounds — a jet of air, a sharp edge and a tube.

The recorder is a familiar type of flute which illustrates this system — the 'jet-edge system' — very clearly.

Inside the beak of a recorder mouthpiece there is a slot-shaped tube called the windway. It is about 3.5 cms. long, 1 cm. wide and 0.25 cm. deep. Air which is blown into one end of the windway is shaped and concentrated and directed across a short gap so that it hits a sharp edge.

Strangely, when the air hits that edge, it doesn't simply split in two. For a brief moment, most of the air goes *over* the edge, and then for a moment it goes *under.* This switching to and fro is extraordinarily rapid; it happens hundreds, even thousands of times every second. The air turbulence which results is modified and amplified by the rest of the instrument and this turbulence is what our ears detect — sound *is* minute and rapid changes in air pressure.

Your flute works on exactly the same principle as the recorder. There is a windway to shape and direct an air-jet, a gap and then an edge to 'split' the air. The windway, however, is not built in to the instrument itself; the flautist forms this between his own lips. The edge to which he directs his breath is the rim of the blow-hole.

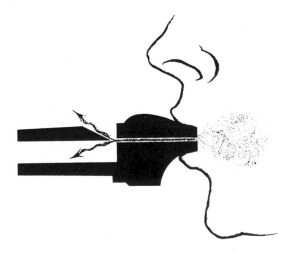

Cross section of a recorder head joint

Cross section of a flute head joint

Shaping the air-jet

One of the most important skills that the flute player has to develop is the ability to shape the windway between his or her lips. The shape of the windway controls the shape, concentration and angling of the air-jet and it is *these* things which largely determine how pleasing a sound you produce, so —

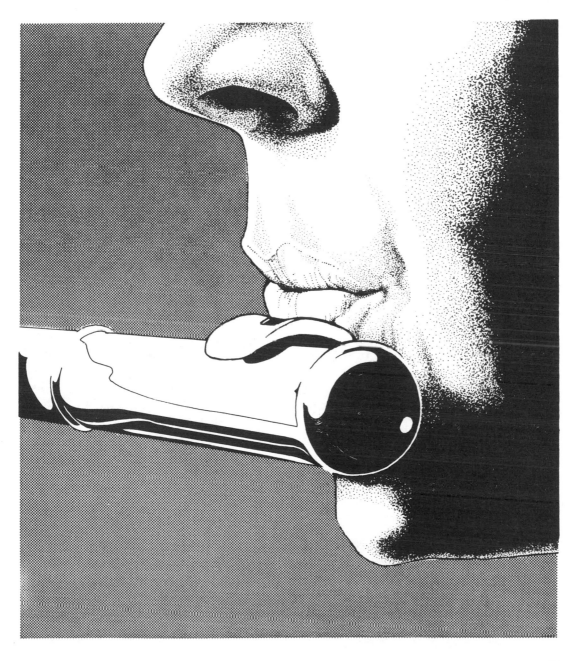

How wide should the air-jet be? — You should aim to make an air-jet which is as wide as the edge that you are blowing against. If the jet is wider than the blow-hole, valuable air will escape to either side and be wasted. If it is narrower, the flute will be quieter than it needs to be.

How deep should the air-jet be? — If you make the air-jet too deep, air will be lost both over and inside the flute and the air will be unconcentrated. Consequently, the tone will be weak and windy. If the air-jet is too shallow (this is less likely for a beginner), the tone will be rather thin and mean and aiming the air might be difficult.

It follows that the air-jet, and therefore the space between your lips, will need to be relatively long and flat(ish) — this sort of shape —

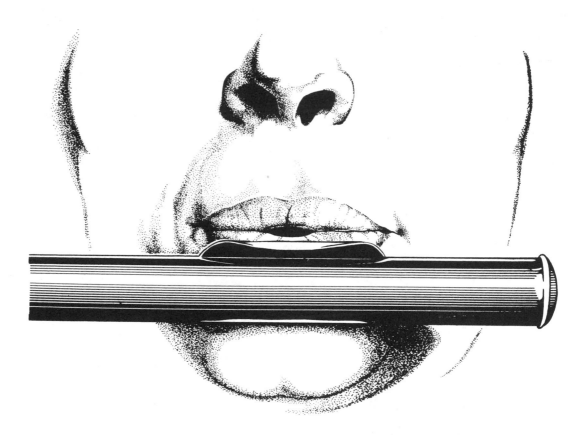

To form this shape, your lips will have to be stretched out to the side a little as if you were saying 'ee', clearly, but not in a forced way. 'Oo' and whistling shapes will give you a lip aperture which is too narrow and too deep — too round, in other words.

How long a gap should there be between the lip opening and the edge? There is no absolute answer to this question because, ideally, the length of the air-jet will need to be varied as you play (shorter for high notes, longer for low notes). However, I can say that for any particular note too long an air-jet will tend to produce a note which sounds too high and has a reasonably loud but rather characterless tone. Too short an air-jet will produce the opposite — a note which sounds too low and muffled. Placing your bottom lip so that it covers about one third of the blow-hole will give you a good, average-length air-jet. You can vary its length by flexing your lips, rather as if you were saying 'eeee - oooo'.

Try to keep these things in mind, and refer back to them if you are having particular problems.

Your lips and the muscles which control them, and their shape and position relative to the flute are known as your EMBOUCHURE (om-boo-sure).

Making the first sound

1.   Take the head joint of the flute — you're better off without the rest for now — and sit or stand in front of a mirror so that you can keep a visual check on what you are doing. Hold the head joint as shown below, with the long part pointing out to your right and your right hand sealing the open end.

2.   Brush the lip plate up your chin, squeezing your bottom lip upwards a little. This is important — use the lip plate to *support* your bottom lip, not to press it back and trap it against your teeth. Line up the blow-hole with the centre of your lips and make sure that the tube runs parallel to your mouth.

Your lower lip should cover about one-third of the blow-hole and should be in contact with the lip plate on both sides of it, so don't pull the lip back and away, but let it 'sit' along the lip plate.

3.   Add a little sideways tension to the lips now ('ee'), place the lips one on top of the other and press them lightly together. Purse the lips a little in the middle and make sure that your teeth are separated.

4.   Now blow, positively, but not hard, allowing the air to part your lips in the middle. It may help to think of saying 'peu. . .'*, but restrain the outer two-thirds of your lips. Make it a long blow, even if there is no sound at first.

* pronounce as in French

Did it work?

If it did, you were lucky. If it didn't, welcome to an enormous club with many distinguished members, and try again. The sound you are after is a fairly low, mellow note, but not with quite the normal flute tone. Here are some of the most likely reasons for your failure: —

1.   Perhaps you were blowing too high or too low and simply missed the edge. You can control the angle of the air-jet by pushing either your top lip or your bottom jaw forwards and backwards. Experiment by blowing on to your hand. Focus a cold spot of air into the centre of your palm and make it travel up and down without moving your head or your hand. Use the same movement to find the right blowing angle when you play the head joint again.

2.   Perhaps the head joint itself wasn't in quite the right place. Check in the mirror to see whether the blow-hole is lined up correctly. And as you blow, roll the hole back towards you and then away again until you find a better position.

3.   Perhaps the air-jet was too thick or wide. Perhaps you were 'ooing' too much. Look in the mirror — see how the shape of your lip opening compares with the illustration above. You'll never get it exactly the same, but it should be similar.

4.   Perhaps your bottom lip was too far forward, or not far forward enough!

10

5. Perhaps you are drawing your lips away from the flute.

6. Lastly, maybe your teeth or tongue were getting in the way. Keep your teeth separated and your tongue low.

Don't be at all surprised if it takes some time to get the hang of all this. It may take minutes, hours, days or weeks, but be patient. Remember that you are asking your lips and the many muscles around your mouth to act, for them, in quite novel combinations.

Keep trying — calmly, and as often as you can — but only for short periods. When you have got the sound — I've never known anyone not get it, if they were determined and patient — try to refine the shape of your lip aperture and the air-jet along the lines I described above. Let the sound be your guide. If it is fuller, stronger and clearer, you must be doing something right.

Carry on working with the head joint until you are satisfied that the sound you are getting is reasonably strong and reliable. Always play long notes — you should be able to sustain one for at least a few seconds. As soon as you can, abandon the 'p' way of starting the sound and try to fix your lips in a position that will produce a good sound before you blow. Practise starting the sound quickly, but without a jolt or a little cough.

While you are busy with that, there are some other things to be thinking about.

Breathing

You will soon discover that the kind of breathing that you use to get yourself through the day isn't deep enough or controlled enough for playing the flute, and you will want to improve the way that you breathe. Deeper breathing will allow you to play more music in one breath — you don't want to be gasping every few notes. Controlled breathing will allow you to play expressively and to develop a beautiful tone. (It will stop you becoming dizzy, too.)

It's useful to understand just what happens when you breathe. Everyone realises that there is a connection between breathing and the rhythmic expansion and contraction of the rib cage which accompanies it, but most people get the connection the wrong way around, thinking that the chest expands because the air that they breathe in pushes their ribs apart, as if their sides were the sides of a balloon. In a funny way, it does actually feel like that, but the reverse is true; air is drawn in *because* you expand your rib cage — the ribs move first.

As you expand your chest, you create spaces inside you — in your lungs — and air rushes in through your nose and mouth to fill those spaces because air is like water and will fill every crack it can whenever it can. At the same time that you move your ribs outwards, you move a large muscle called the diaphragm downwards, thus creating even more room in your lungs. Your diaphragm is situated under your lungs and above your stomach.

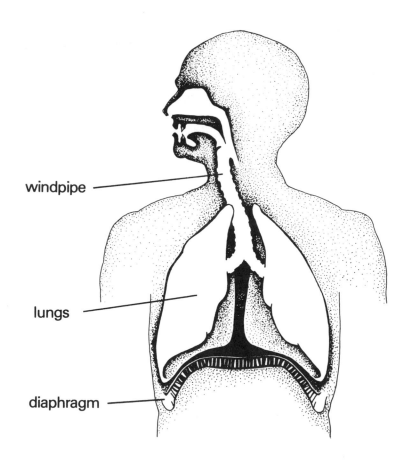

windpipe

lungs

diaphragm

When most people breathe, they hardly use their diaphragms at all and make only small movements with their ribs. As a result, only a quarter of the potential capacity of the lungs is used. Every flute player has to get into the habit of breathing more deeply than this, making full use of the rib cage *and* the diaphragm. Avoid military style deep breathing in which the shoulders are raised, the chest puffed out and the tummy sucked in. That might look impressive but the lower, larger parts of the lungs are actually being *de*flated. If the diaphragm is used well, your stomach, back and sides will all bulge outwards as well as your chest. The shoulders shouldn't move.

Try taking a deep breath now. Try to fill your lungs from the bottom upwards. If you rest your hands on your waist, they should be pushed apart.

The flute player often needs to take deep breaths quickly and quietly, and always has the problem of controlling the breath as it is exhaled — in a sense, that *is* flute playing. Here is a breathing exercise especially designed to develop these, and other essential abilities. You can practise it anywhere and at any time, but always do it before you play the flute. It will put you in mind of good breathing habits and improve your strength and control. It will also help to calm you before you play.

Standing or sitting up straight to allow your lungs to expand fully:

1.   Breathe in — very deeply — over about three seconds. Make sure that your throat is wide open, as it is when you yawn, so that the air can enter quietly and quickly.

2.   Hold your breath for 5-10 seconds. Don't block your throat or close your mouth when you do this. With the lungs still full, pant like a dog, but making as little sound as possible (indicating that your throat is as open as possible).

This part of the exercise will strengthen the muscles that open your lungs, increase your capacity and teach you to control your diaphragm — those little jabs that you make while panting will be very useful later.

3.   Breathe out over about 10 seconds with the throat still open, attempting to maintain an even, level flow of air from start to finish. You will hear just how even your breath is, of course, if you play a note as you exhale. Resist a loud start and a trail-off finish and don't cave in to squeeze out every last drop of air; stop when it feels natural to do so.

4.   Rest and repeat.

When you can do the whole cycle smoothly and comfortably, decrease the time spent on 1, increase the time spent on 2, and vary the time for 3, sometimes allowing the air to pour out on its own, sometimes forcing it out as rapidly as possible. Eventually repeat the whole thing three or four times without resting.

How music is written down

Below, you will see how written music tells you which notes to play and how long they should last. These are the two things that you need to know more than any others if you want to find out how a piece of music 'goes'.

Don't be put off if what you read seems confusing, complicated or even pure gobbledygook at first. The logic, simplicity and sense of it all will become clear when you use the system, and you'll be going through it all bit by bit later in the book. For the moment, take in what you can and refer back to this section as the need arises.

THE NOTES

By pressing different combinations of keys and blowing in particular ways, you can produce about 40 notes from your flute, each one an equal step higher than the last. If you were to play the lowest of these notes and then each of the twelve above it in turn, you would come, at the end of the twelve, to a note which sounded strikingly similar to the first note, even though it was obviously higher, and therefore different.

If this seems a strange idea, remember that if a large crowd of people sing a song together — a hymn, a protest song or the national anthem, for instance — then, although it is true to say that everyone is singing the same notes, it is also true to say that, on the whole, the women and children sing these notes in higher voices than the men; they sing the same notes, but higher; the men sing the same notes, but lower; the same — *but different*! The distance, or *interval* between two notes which are the-same-but-different is called an *octave.* You can experience how large that interval is by singing the first two notes of '*Some-where* over the rainbow'.

To simplify the naming of notes, all notes separated by the interval of an octave (or two octaves, or three etc.) are given the same name. In consequence, we don't need 40 names for the notes on your flute, because the 30 or so that you haven't 'played' are just higher versions of the original 12.

To simplify matters further, the basic 12 notes are named after only the first seven letters of the alphabet. Seven of the 12 have straightforward names — A, B, C etc. (going up.) The other five fit in between some of the seven 'naturals' and each one has two possible names, borrowed in part from the notes on either side. For instance, the note between A and B is higher than A but lower than B, so it can be called 'A sharp' ('sharp' means 'higher than') or 'B flat' ('flat' means 'lower than') depending purely on which is more convenient.

14

Perhaps the diagram below will help you to visualise this more clearly. It shows a never-ending staircase of equally-sized steps. Each represents a note higher or lower than the last. Once around (12 steps) takes you up or down an octave to one of those same-but-different notes. If you carry on you come to all the same notes again, but each time in a higher or lower octave.

The interval between notes on adjacent steps is called a *semitone* (E to F, for instance). A two-step interval (such as F to G) is called a *tone*.

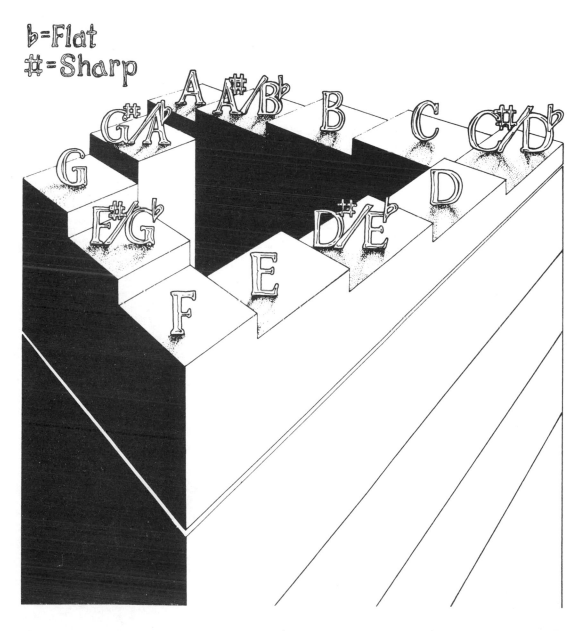

To indicate which of these notes a musician should play, the round part of one of these symbols

is placed in the appropriate position on the *stave*, five horizontal lines containing four spaces. Each line and each space is reserved for one letter name:

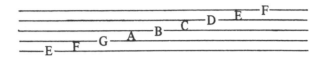

It's easy to remember the letters in the spaces; going up, they spell FACE. Most people remember EGBDF (the notes on the lines) by making up a sentence such as *E*very *G*ood *B*oy *D*eserves *F*ootball or *E*skimos *G*oing *B*elly *D*ancing *F*reeze. The sillier the better.

This example, then, would tell you to play C, B, G, F.

To indicate sharps and flats, these signs are put before notes: ♯ = sharp; ♭ = flat. The next example would tell you to play C sharp, B flat, G sharp and F sharp.

(The squiggly sign at the start of the last two examples is a *Treble Clef*. You will see one at the start of all flute music but you needn't worry about its significance.)

The F written in the bottom space of the stave is not any F; it is the lowest available on your flute. The F on the top line is the F an octave higher.

Clearly, some notes will be too high or low to fit on the stave, but extra lines (leger lines) can be added above and below to accommodate them. Here are all the notes that you will come across in this book, and their positions on, above and below the stave. Notice that a rise or fall of one letter name always means a move from 'in a space' to 'on a line' or vice-versa.

16

Whether the stem of a note points up or down does not affect the pitch of the note.

C D E F G A B C D E F G A B C D E

THE RHYTHM

At the heart of almost every piece of music is a *pulse*. When you tap your foot or dance 'in time' it is this pulse that you are marking. It might go at any speed; in lively music it is usually quick; in more reflective music it tends to be slow. Quick or slow, however, it consists of distinct and *evenly-spaced* points in time. We call it *the beat*.

Try clapping a steady beat. Listen hard for imperfections in its evenness. Does it slow down or speed up? Do some claps come a fraction early or late? Try out different speeds.

The beat in music is there because we enjoy it. But its presence is also very useful because it gives us a way of defining the length of any note. A little confusingly, perhaps, the length of time from one pulse to the next is called *a* beat (rather than *the* beat) and this is the basic unit of musical time. We can say that a note is one beat long, five beats long, two-and-a-half beats long, and so on. The length of one beat will remain constant throughout any particular piece, but will vary from one piece to another, depending on the speed of the underlying pulse.

A special set of symbols is used to indicate notes of different lengths. You have already seen how the positioning of these symbols on the stave can show you which note to play, but it is the shape of each symbol which tells you how long that note should last.

Two sets of names are in use for these symbols. I find the 'fraction' names more sensible and they seem to be being used more and more commonly, but both sets of names are given here, and it is as well to know both:

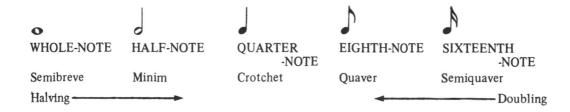

WHOLE-NOTE	HALF-NOTE	QUARTER -NOTE	EIGHTH-NOTE	SIXTEENTH -NOTE
Semibreve	Minim	Crotchet	Quaver	Semiquaver

Halving ⟶   ⟵ Doubling

None of the above symbols indicates a fixed number of beats. For each piece that he writes down, a composer will choose one of them (almost always one of the middle three) to indicate a note with a length of one beat. He will then use the symbol to its left to mean two beats, the one to the left of that to mean four, and so on. The symbols to the right of the one beat note will indicate half a beat, a quarter, an eighth, etc. As you can see, the lengths of notes are relative, not fixed, and work by doubling (towards the left) and halving (towards the right).

This table shows how the value in beats of each symbol changes when different symbols are chosen to represent one beat.

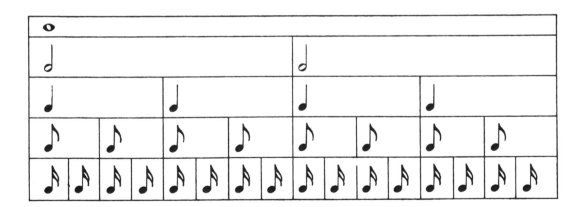

And from this table you can see how many notes of any kind are needed to equal the time taken up by any other:

Music contains silences as well as sounds, and these too have to be measured. Special symbols called *rests* are used and are equivalent in length to the notes that you have already seen.

By the way, notes of intermediate lengths such as three beats or one-and-a-half beats can be written by 'tying' or 'dotting' notes. You will see how these techniques work later in the book.

BARS

Most music is based on a pulse, but it is a pulse with a regularly placed accent in it.

Clap a regular pulse. Check it for evenness. Then make some claps louder than others like this:

1) Every THIRD clap louder —

	CLAP	clap	clap	CLAP	clap	clap	etc.
Count:	"1	2	3	1	2	3"	etc.

2) Every FOURTH clap louder —

CLAP	clap	clap	clap	CLAP	clap	clap	clap	CLAP	clap	clap	clap
"1	2	3	4	1	2	3	4	1	2	3	4

The time from one accented beat to the next is called a *bar* or *measure*. In example 1) above, we say that there are three beats to a bar. In example 2) there are four beats to a bar.

GOD SAVE THE QUEEN has three beats to the bar. Clap as you did in example 1) and sing 'God save our gra — cious Queen' along with it, with 'God' on a loud clap. The accented clapping and the tune should fit naturally together.

GOOD KING WENCESLAS has four beats to the bar.

Sing:	Good	King	Wen —	ces —	las	looked	out,		On	the
Clap:	*	*	*	*	*	*	*	*	*	*

Again, you will hear that the natural accents in the tune come around at regular intervals and coincide with your clapping. In some tunes the natural accents are three beats apart, sometimes four, but they may also be two, five, six, seven, *etc.*

For ease of reading, all the notes which are to be played between one accented beat and the next are written on the stave between two vertical lines called bar-lines. It is the first note after each bar-line which is stressed.

God	rest	you	me-rry	gen-tle-men,	let	nothing you dis-may	for	Je-
1	2	3	4	1 2 3 4		1 2 3 4	1 2 3 etc.	

Note that there need not be the same number of notes in every bar, but that, however many notes there are, they always occupy the same total amount of time.

THE TIME SIGNATURE

At the beginning of every piece of music you will see what looks like a fraction. This is the *time signature*. The top number tells you how many beats to a bar there are in the piece, so this gives you the chance to count a few bars to yourself and get the feel of the underlying rhythm before you start. The lower number tells you what kind of note is going to be used to indicate one beat. Here are some examples of common time signatures:

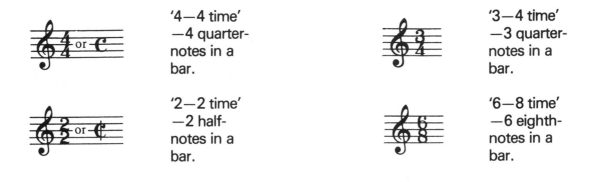

'4—4 time'
—4 quarter-notes in a bar.

'3—4 time'
—3 quarter-notes in a bar.

'2—2 time'
—2 half-notes in a bar.

'6—8 time'
—6 eighth-notes in a bar.

You may also find a *tempo* indication. This tells you how fast or slow the music should go. The tempo indication might take the form of a *metronome mark* which gives you the speed of the music in beats, or sometimes bars, per minute, *e.g.* ♩ = 72. All the pieces in this book have metronome markings.

There is no need to play at EXACTLY the speed given. Treat the markings as a rough guide and play the pieces at a speed which sounds right to you. In other music you might see Italian or French words at the start. These often tell you whether the music should be fast or slow and you will find a list of these and their meanings on p 101.

Reading Music

Understanding how music is written down is one thing. *Reading* music — turning what you see into sound — is another.

If you are going to have any difficulties reading music — you probably won't, but *if* you do — then they will almost certainly have to do with the rhythm rather than the notes. Many people find that neither the notes nor the rhythm are difficult on their own, but that when they combine them, one puts them off the other.

To get round this problem, I offer you the method below. If you use it carefully, you should soon be able to abandon it bit by bit. If you don't use it, you could be guessing, and playing very curious music for ever.

First of all, deal with the rhythm of the piece. Let's say that this:

is the piece that you want to play. Look at the time signature. It is in 4—4 time. That means that there are going to be four beats in a bar, counted 1 2 3 4 1 2 3 4 *etc.,* and that a quarter note is going to last for one beat — the time from one count to the next.

Next, look at the music and decide on which beat of the bar each note should start. In bars 1 and 3 of our piece, all the notes are quarter notes which last for one beat each, so in both cases the first quarter-note starts on 1 and fills up all the time until the second beat. The next note, then, starts on 2, the third one on 3 and the fourth on 4. Write the numbers underneath the notes.

In bars 2 and 4 there are some half-notes. Half-notes last for twice as many beats as quarter-notes, so here they last for two beats each. In bar 4, the first half-note fills up the time from 1 to 2 (that's one beat), PLUS the time from 2 to 3 (that makes two). The second half-note starts where the last note left off, on 3, and lasts until the 1 of the next bar.

The complete four bars should be numbered like this. (Write the beats where nothing new happens in brackets.)

1 2 3 4   1 2 3 (4)   1 2 3 4   1 (2) 3 (4)

The rest is easy.

Next, count evenly and steadily at a speed which feels natural and comfortable — '1 2 3 4 1 2 3 4' etc. and clap, but only on those counts where a note starts, i.e. the ones which aren't in brackets.

IMPORTANT — you are 500% less likely to go wrong at this stage if you count *out loud*. Try it. It should go like this:

Clap	*	*	*	*	*	*	*		*	*	*	*	*		*
Count	1	2	3	4	1	2	3	(4)	1	2	3	4	1	(2)	3	(4)

Then do the same again, but this time, just whispering or clearly mouthing the counts as you clap. Now you should be able to hear your clapping better.

Then, if that is going well, just **think** the numbers as you clap. Don't lose the steadiness of the beat; tap your foot if that helps. Keep repeating this stage until you know how the rhythm goes.

You should recognise the rhythm that you are clapping. It's a Christmas carol. Its title is over the page but don't look until you're sure.

Now get to know the notes. Ignore the rhythm; just play through the notes again and again until you can do it quite quickly, and until they hold no surprises for you.

Now revise the rhythm.

Finally, play the rhythm that you now know so well, using the notes that you have already rehearsed. Don't let anything put you off the rhythm. Accept wrong notes, no notes, shrieks and raspberries at this stage, so long as you get the rhythm right. Remember — use the notes as something to play the rhythm with — the 'tune' will appear as if by magic.

Here it is again. I suggest you copy this out and stick it to your music stand. Learn each piece a phrase at a time (from breath mark to breath mark).

22

1. Number the music.
2. Count **out loud** all the beats of the bar, and clap on the beats where a new note starts.
3. The same, but whispering.
4. The same, but thinking (hard), until you know the rhythm.
5. Rehearse the notes.
6. Revise the rhythm.
7. Use the notes to play the rhythm.

If you don't feel confident of your ability to clap or count regularly, buy or borrow a metronome, or make a tape of yourself counting and then clap and play along with that.

Holding the Flute

Your flute will be easier to play and your playing more effective if you learn how to stand and hold your flute efficiently. Study this picture carefully. Note that the arms are raised to allow deeper breathing and better access to the keys, and that the head is held up and the trunk and throat

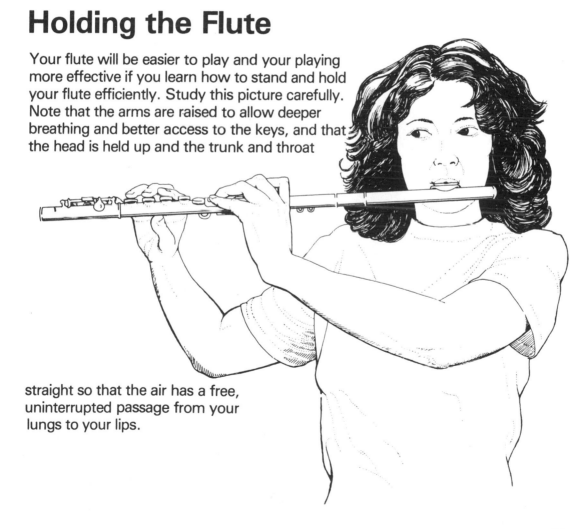

straight so that the air has a free, uninterrupted passage from your lungs to your lips.

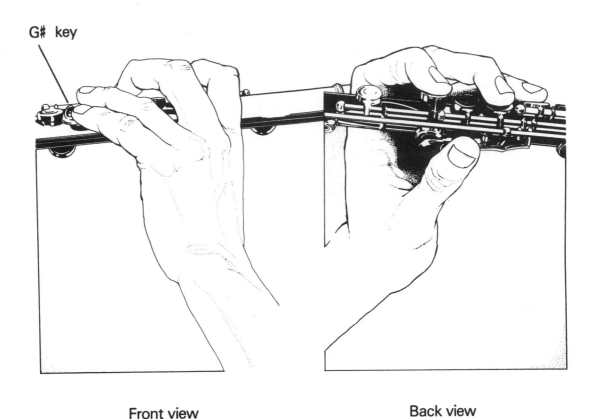

G# key

Front view

Back view

THE LEFT HAND

Notice that there should be an empty key to both sides of your index finger, and that your thumb should for the moment press the larger of the two thumb keys. Your first finger should be bent, the second less so and the third almost straight. Your little finger should be able to reach the 'G♯ key' without stretching. The side of the first joint of your index finger should press against the flute, pushing it back towards you.

(The rhythm you were clapping was **GOOD KING WENCESLAS**.)

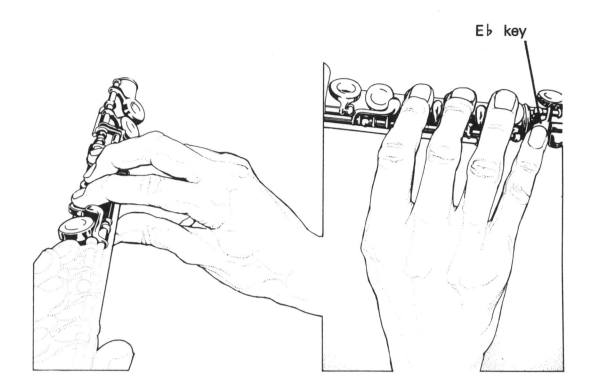

Looking along the flute from the head joint   Looking down on the right hand

THE RIGHT HAND

The first, second and third fingers of your right hand press the three large keys nearest the foot joint. They should approach the flute more or less at right angles and be slightly curved so that the fingertips can press the **centres** of the keys **without these fingers otherwise touching the flute at all**. The little finger should press the E♭ key almost all the time, and your thumb should be positioned underneath your first finger.

The flautist needs to hold the flute absolutely steady at all times but also needs to leave as many fingers as possible completely free to press and release the keys with maximum efficiency. The solution to this problem is:

at all times, push the flute away from you with the little finger and thumb of your right hand and push the flute **towards** you with the side of your left index finger. If the lip plate is against your chin, this combination of forces should be all that is needed to support and steady the flute.

I can't say this strongly enough. Learn to use this grip now, and many considerable problems that you might have had in the future simply won't arise.

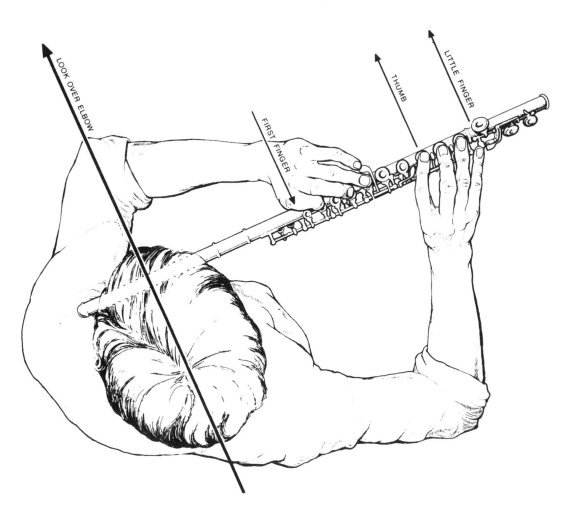

Fingering Diagrams

You will find fingering diagrams scattered throughout this book. They show you which combinations of keys you should press in order to obtain different notes. The picture below shows how the circles etc., in the diagrams, correspond to the keys on your flute. Notice that only the keys which are actually pressed are incorporated into the diagrams. (The numbers on the flute keys show where your fingers go. 1 = your index finger.)

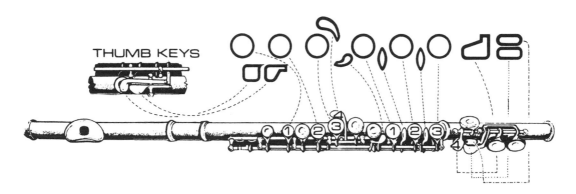

Keys which aren't often used are generally omitted from fingering diagrams and a line is inserted to separate the left hand keys from the right hand keys. That leaves you with this:

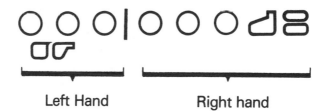

The keys to be pressed are filled in; ●
The others are left open: ○

The left thumb has two keys to press.

  ◖◗ = press the left ('B flat') key.
  ◖◗ = press the right ('B natural') key.
  ◗ = press either.

PART TWO
Playing the Flute

Sip the next part of the book. Don't gulp! Take it one bit at a time and in the right order. Don't miss anything out and do your best with each new piece or idea before you move on to the next.

I hope that you will enjoy the tunes in the next section. These will all sound fine played on their own, but to make them even more enjoyable, ask a friend or your teacher to play the guitar or piano accompaniments which you will find in the detachable supplement. (Many pianists will be able to make sense of the guitar chords, by the way.) Always be on the lookout for pieces similar to the ones that you find in this book; to learn to read music fluently you will need to play lots of tunes with similar rhythms and so on — more than there could be room for in one book. By the time you reach page 72 it will be easy to find new pieces that you can play. Investigate recorder music as well as flute music.

Lastly, writers of some instrumental tutors bravely promise instant results. I don't! Practice, over a period of time — as I'm sure you realise — is the only way to achieve worthwhile results. This doesn't mean hours a day, or even every day, although regularity is certainly important. At first, two or three 10-minute sessions each day are best. If you can't manage that, don't worry, but don't go too long without playing because the things that you have learned will come 'unstuck'. Later on, make your sessions longer, but never so long that you become tired or lose your concentration.

Practise purposefully and ask yourself these questions now and then (answer honestly!)

Grip — are you holding your flute in the best way possible?

Tone — does every note sound as beautiful as you can make it at the moment? (Improving your tone is a slow but rewarding process.)

Fingering — are you using the best possible, complete fingering for every note, and when you change from one fingering to the next, do your fingers move quickly and together?

Rhythm — have you troubled to read the rhythm accurately? Never guess.

Phrasing — (You'll see what this means later) — are you following the phrasing in the music exactly?

Breathing — do you always breathe deeply? Is your throat always open? Don't forget the breathing exercise.

Perhaps this is something else to copy out and stick to your music stand?

Good luck. Take your time. Have fun.

So long as you can produce a reasonably clear sound on the head joint, you should now move on to playing the complete flute.

When the flute is assembled correctly (see page 4), place all your fingers on the appropriate keys (see page 26) and bring the lip plate to your bottom lip just as you did when you practised with the head joint alone. Now that you aren't actually holding the head joint, you may find it harder to control. Do use a mirror.

Remember to support your bottom lip — don't squash it. And check in the mirror that everything is lined up as it should be and that your 'grip' is correct.

Press forward with your right thumb and little finger. The head joint should press back against your chin.

Now, except for the thumb and first finger of your left hand, and the thumb and little finger of your right hand — they're the ones doing the pressing — raise all your fingers, just enough to open the keys. The fingering that you have been left with should be this —

This is the fingering for B. As you can see, B is written on the centre line of the stave.

It may take a few moments now to position and angle the blow-hole so that it is just as it was when you blew the head joint alone, but when you have found the sound again, try the simple exercise below.

The exercise is in 4-time, so you should count four beats in a bar. Count evenly at a speed which feels natural and unhurried.

Each of the whole-notes (semibreves) lasts for four beats — a complete bar — so start playing on 1 and then sustain the sound right through 2, 3 and 4 until the moment you think '1' again.

The quarter-note (crotchet) rests last for one count each.

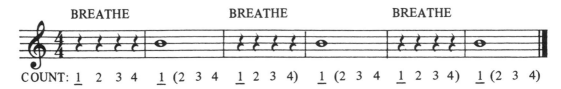

COUNT: 1 2 3 4   1 (2 3 4   1 2 3 4)   1 (2 3 4   1 2 3 4)   1 (2 3 4)

Here is the fingering for A. Be sure to put your second finger on the right key — not the one next to your first finger, but the one next to that.

The next exercise involves A and B and includes some quarter-notes (crotchets) which last for one beat each.

So that you can breathe without disrupting the rhythm you will have to cut the whole-notes (semibreves) short by breathing on 4 where you see this sign — ✔

Breathe deeply through an open throat and blow smoothly through one note and into the next.

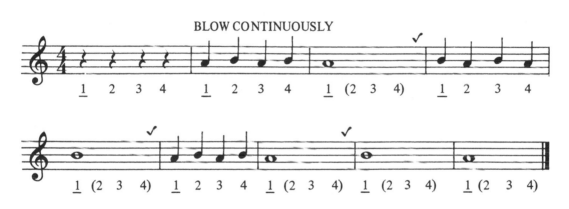

Here is something just a little more complex. Be sure to clap and count the rhythm first. (see page 21)

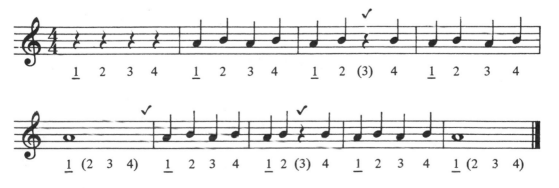

Add the third finger of your left hand to the A fingering and you will have the fingering for G.

(Notice that to produce lower notes you press more keys, effectively making the closed section of the flute tube longer. The longer the tube, the lower the note.)

The three little pieces which follow use only B, A and G. Two of them have accompaniments for someone else to play, either on another melody instrument or a guitar. Check that the instrument you are playing *with* is at *concert pitch* — your accompanist will know what that means — and ask him or her to play you an A to compare with your own. The two notes should sound the same. If your A sounds too high, move your bottom lip a little further over the blow-hole or roll the flute in a little — as if it were rolling up towards your nose. Use whichever method produces the best sound, or a combination of both. And make the opposite movements if your A is too low.

When you know how this next piece goes, try playing it to a quicker — but still steady — beat. In places you will need to move two fingers at the same time. Make sure that they are well synchronised and that they move quickly.

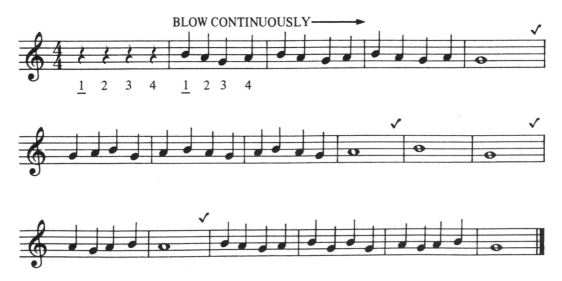

Check on the way that you breathe and blow as you play this next piece. Blow positively, turning the pressure up to full right from the start (without 'coughing'), and have your lips in position before you blow.

The two dots at the end of the piece tell you to repeat the music that you have just played. Remember to 'count yourself in'.

THE SEVENTH NIGHT

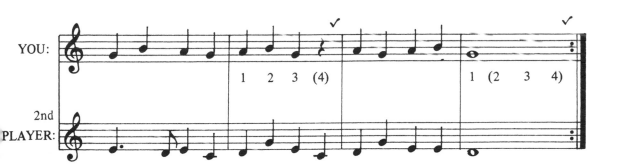

Prepare the rhythm of the next piece carefully. The bars with brackets and 1 and 2 written over them are 'first and second time endings'. End the piece with bar '1' the first time but **omit** it on the repetition and play bar '2' instead. In this piece, your own part isn't affected, but the second part is.

STREAKED WITH JEWELS

The Slur

A slur is a curved line written under or over a group of notes. It looks like this:

and all the notes covered by a slur should sound smoothly connected. So far as the flute player is concerned this simply means blowing continuously and evenly as you change fingerings (which is something I've been encouraging you to do anyway). Such smooth playing is termed *legato* and you say that notes are 'slurred' together.

Try to follow the slurs and breath marks in this book very closely. If you get into the habit of breathing more or less anywhere or, even worse, using a separate puff for each note, you will find that the music ceases to flow and make sense. If you desperately need to breathe in the middle of a slurred group of notes, the *least* musical place to do so is almost always at the end of a bar. As a general rule, the best places to breathe are the same places in which you would breathe instinctively if you were singing rather than playing a piece.

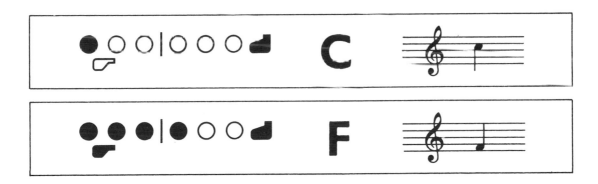

Here are two more notes, one lower and one higher than the notes that you already know. F brings your right hand into action, so if the right hand fingers have been resting on the flute, now is the time to lift them. They should be hovering over the keys, ready for action. Except for pressing the keys, the first three fingers of the right hand shouldn't touch the flute at all.

There is a whole-note (semibreve) rest in the next piece. Otherwise, you should find no surprises.

ILKERTON RIDGE

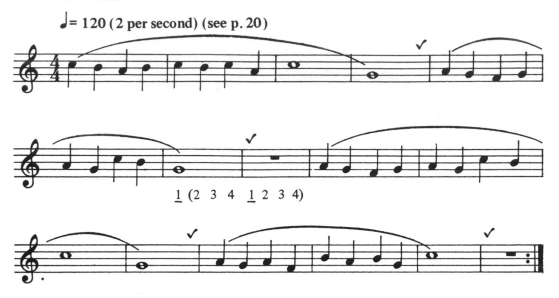

♩ = 120 (2 per second) (see p. 20)

1 (2 3 4 1 2 3 4)

There's a Hungarian flavour to the next piece. It should go gracefully at about 100 beats per minute — a little slower than 2 per second. A second player can play this:

over and over while you play the tune.

LYDIAN SONG

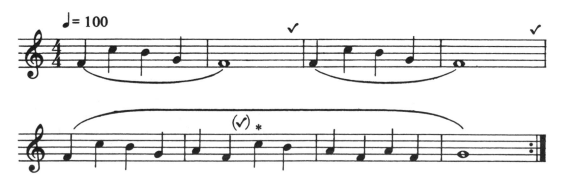

♩ = 100

*(✔) means 'this is a musical place to breathe if you **have** to.'

36

Half-notes or Minims

As you saw on page 18, and as you might expect, a half-note *(minim)* lasts for twice as many beats as a quarter-note *(crotchet),* so where a quarter-note lasts for one-beat, a half-note will last for two.

Half-notes look like this:

and you should count them as follows:

<u>1</u> (2) 3 4   1 2 3 (4)   1 2 (3) 4   1 (2) 3 (4)

(Clap and count each bar over and over, without breaking the beat at all. Then try all four bars one after the other.)

Here is a piece which includes some half-notes:

THE CARP

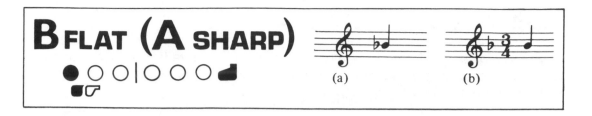

B FLAT (A SHARP)

(a) (b)

Another new note, this time with two alternative names. It fits in between A and B — play A, B flat, B to *hear* how it fits — so it can either be called B♭ (♭ = flat) or A♯ (♯ = sharp). Look at page 14 again if this doesn't make sense.

For the moment, we'll call the new note B♭ .

If a B♭ occurs in a piece where B♮ (♮ = *natural* — the *ordinary* B) is more commonly used, it will be written as a B, but with a flat sign in front of it, as in example (a) above. In this case, the sign is known as an *accidental* and it applies to any subsequent Bs in the same bar, but not beyond. The same applies to any flat, sharp or natural sign which appears in the middle of a piece, whatever note it is attached to.

If, on the other hand, B♭ is going to be used throughout a piece, a flat sign is put at the start of the music, on the B line and before the time signature, (example (b)). Then the sign is called the *key signature* and tells you to play B♭ *whenever* you see a note on the B line. (By the way, the 'key' in key signature has nothing to do with the keys on your flute.)

As a general rule, *whenever* B♭ *is in the key signature, put your left thumb on the* B♭ *key and leave it there* except for notes like C where the thumb needs to be raised. No other notes will be affected by pressing this key and it's a good idea not to switch your thumb backwards and forwards unnecessarily.

Be careful with the repeat marks in this piece.

𝄇 = somewhere to return *from*.

𝄆 = the point to return *to*.

𝄇 = go back to the last 𝄆 unless there isn't one, in which case you should go back to the very beginning.

RONDE

SUSATO (adapted)

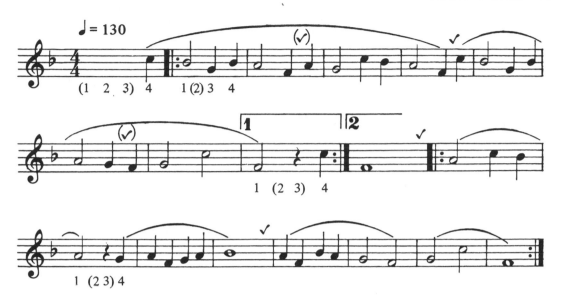

The title of this piece is printed over the page. Try to work out what it is before you look.

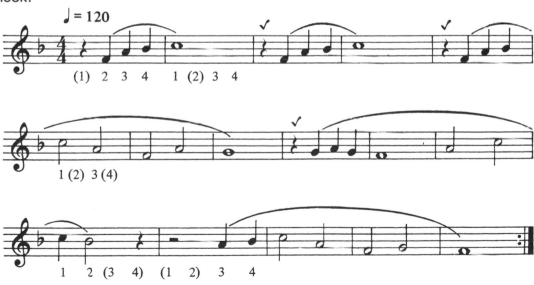

The next piece has B flats and B naturals in it. To avoid moving your thumb, use this alternative fingering for B flat and keep your thumb on the natural key.

This piece is a 'canon', which means that a second player can play the same music as you, but starting later, when you get to "2".

CANON

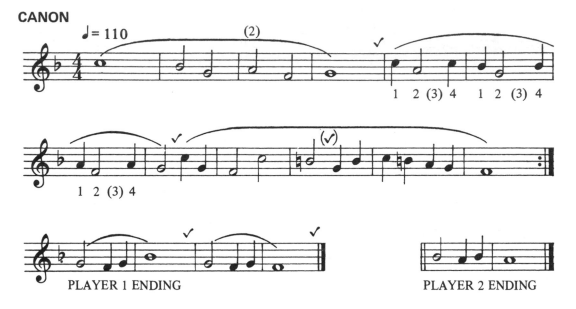

(The untitled piece on page 39 is **WHEN THE SAINTS GO MARCHING IN**.)

Centreing the Flute

Now that you know a few notes, it will be worth devoting some time to improving the sound that you make.

The first step towards getting the best possible sound from your flute is to check and adjust the positioning of the blow-hole edge relative to the air-jet. For the best results, the air that leaves your lips should be perfectly aligned with the edge, striking its entire length at right angles like this:

Check on all the different alignments shown below by playing a note while you move the flute to and fro — very slowly — in each of the directions shown, one at a time. In each case, you should find a central position that works better than any other.

USE THESE MOVEMENTS
TO CORRECT THESE ALIGNMENTS

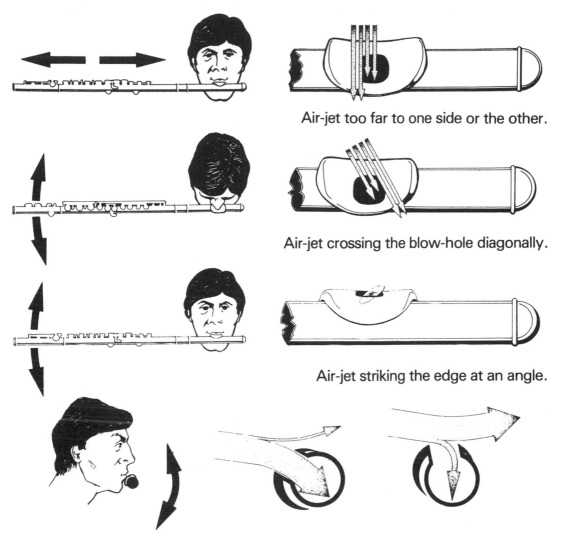

Air-jet too far to one side or the other.

Air-jet crossing the blow-hole diagonally.

Air-jet striking the edge at an angle.

Air-jet unevenly divided, and perhaps too long or too short.

The last movement is particularly important because, as you will hear when you try it, it affects not only the tone but also the tuning of the flute. Happily, the centred position gives the best tone *and* the best tuning.

You should find it fruitful to experiment with the last movement in combination with varied bottom lip positions.

Add centreing the flute to your practice routine. You will soon find that the centred position feels quite natural.

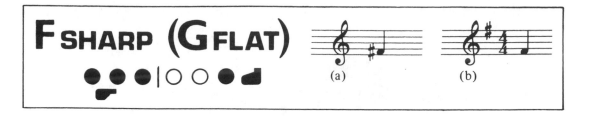

F SHARP (G FLAT)

F♯/G♭ fits between F and G. It is most often known as F♯.

Its use can be indicated either by putting an accidental before an F (a) or by putting a sharp sign on the **upper** F-line of the stave at the start of the music (b).

This next piece has F♯ all the way through. Remember to centre the flute before you start.

WELL-SUNG SONG

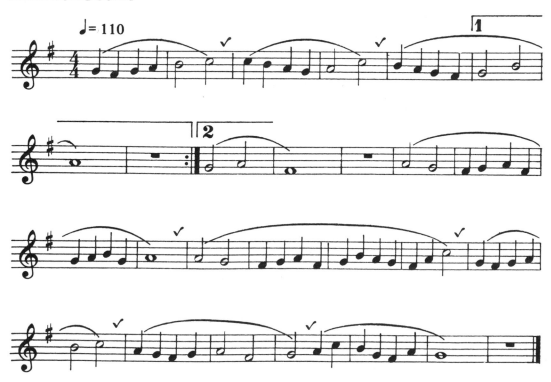

Most, but not all of the Fs in the next piece are sharpened, while the key signature tells you to use B♭s throughout.

INCANTATION

Tonguing

So far, I have encouraged you to blow uninterrupted streams of air so that you will produce unbroken strings of sound. Although this is a good, musical habit to form, music would sound dull if every note in every piece was played in the same way, and you will find that different ways of starting, shaping and finishing notes will add life, style and expression to your playing.

The most important of these forms of 'articulation' is tonguing. This simply means saying 'te' or 'dh' as you start a note. The effect should be a strong beginning to the note, caused by the sudden release of air previously held back by the tongue.

Don't let phrases like 'strong beginning' and 'sudden release' give you the wrong idea; the movement of your tongue should be as quick and light as if you were saying 'titanic' or 'pterodactyl' and bringing your tongue to the roof of your mouth needn't cause an appreciable gap between notes. In the exercise below, 'tongue' every note. **Don't stop blowing** except to breathe.

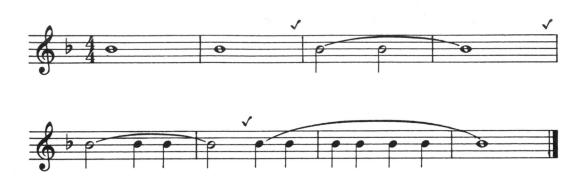

In flute music, a note should be tongued
(a) if it is the first note of a slurred group,
(b) if it is a repeated note within a slurred group,
(c) if it isn't part of a slurred group at all.

This example shows all three possibilities:

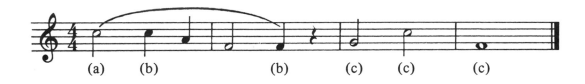

In the case of repeated slurred notes (b), tonguing is necessary simply in order to announce the start of the second note and should therefore be gentle — just interrupt a smooth flow of air with 'dh' (no sound in the throat).

For the slightly stronger effect generally required for (a) and (c) momentarily increase the breath pressure to accompany the tongue action ('t'). No extra effort is needed from the tongue.

In the piece that follows, all the right places to tongue have been marked. That part of music which tells you how to play the notes — whether to tongue or slur them, for instance, is the *phrasing.* Always try to follow the phrasing closely.

TETE-A-TETE

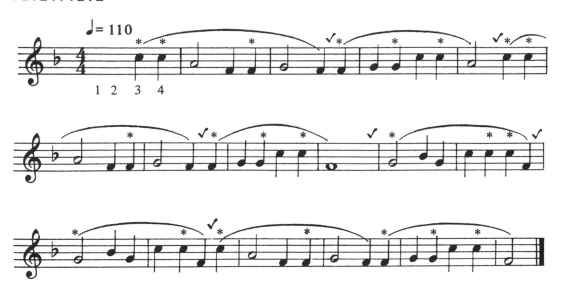

E is your lowest note yet. On its own it shouldn't present any special problems but you will almost certainly find it quite difficult to change from E to F♯ and back without extra notes and hiccups sounding between the ones that you intended. This is because one finger has to go down as two come up. To ease this problem, keep your fingers very close to the keys, or even touching them, at all times. And when you do move your fingers, even — especially — in slow music, move them quickly and deliberately, like a robot's fingers.

The E to F♯ problem doesn't occur in this piece, so you can pay special attention to tonguing well, and in the right places.

WE SHALL NOT BE MOVED

The E to F♯ problem *does* occur in this piece.

THEME FROM BEETHOVEN'S "CHORAL FANTASIA"

The Tie

A 'tie' is simply a special kind of slur. A slur normally indicates that you should connect two or more different notes smoothly. A tie, which looks just the same, indicates that you should do the same thing to two notes at the *same* pitch — two Es or two As, for instance. The effect and the idea of slurring or 'tying' two such notes together is to produce one note as long as the two written notes added together. For example, if you tie these two Bs together, you will hear one B, but three beats long:

Any length of note can be written by tying notes of different values together. Tied notes can be held from one bar to the next and can also be included in groups of notes which are already slurred.

These few bars show all these possibilities. Although you can see 15 notes, you should only hear 11.

Learn pieces which include tied notes like this:
1)   Play all the written notes as if the ties weren't there at all.
*2)   When you are absolutely sure of the underlying rhythm, then **think** each tied note, but don't mark it in any way, just keep blowing.*

There are one or two ties in this Spanish tune. You can play it on your own or with a guitar/piano playing the chords OR with another melody instrument playing in canon (starting when you get to 2) AND/OR another player playing two notes lower or six notes higher than you (starting on an F instead of an A).

DE LOS ALAMOS VENGO

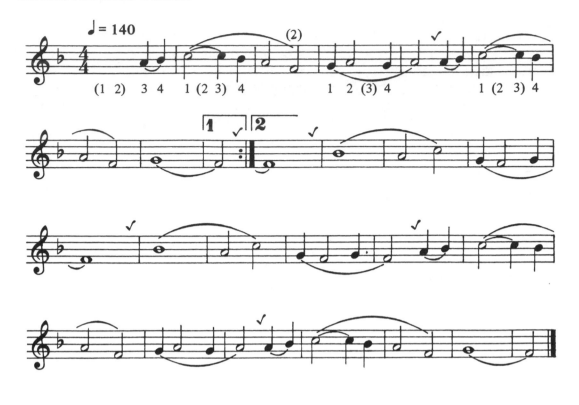

THE SUN AND THE MOON is also adapted from a Spanish folk song.

THE SUN AND THE MOON   **SPANISH TRAD. (adapted)**

These two new notes are an octave apart (see page 14) so they have the same name.

The higher D should be easy to play, but don't be surprised if the lower one is a little reluctant at first. Working down to it — G — F — E — D — might help for the moment. (More help is on the way.)

You will have to master two tricky fingering changes involving these two notes. C to D is awkward because more or less every finger that's up has to go down and vice-versa.

D to E is also tricky because the third and little fingers of your right hand have to move in opposite directions. You will find them less than enthusiastic.

 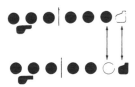

Rehearse both of these tricky changes, and any others that you come across, as follows:

1)   As you play one of the notes, *imagine* the fingering for the other.
2)   When you know exactly what you're going to do — take all the time you need — change to that other fingering, blowing through from one note to the other so that you can *hear* how well coordinated your fingers are.
3)   Change back in the same way. Imagine — *change*.

4)   When you can manage the changes cleanly, start playing 'in time' — play each note for four beats (one beat per second). When you need to breathe, let it be in the middle of the four, but never on the change.

5)   Now make the changes more frequent, first of all by counting only three beats for each note, then only two, then only one, and thereafter by carefully accelerating the beat. Don't rush from one stage to the next. Stay in control.

Try out your C to D change in this tune:

ODE TO JOY   **BEETHOVEN - Slightly simplified**

CHORALE MELODY is a very old tune which has been used by many composers. Bach used it in the 'St. Matthew Passion.' Paul Simon used it for 'American Tune'. Try to make it sound **big**.

CHORALE MELODY

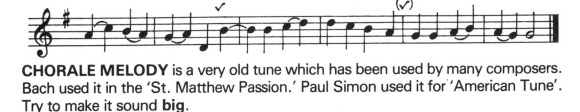

Some help with the lower notes

The sound of your flute spreads out in all directions at about 760 m.p.h. It spreads to your left and your right. It travels upwards and downwards and bounces off the ceiling and the floor. It goes forwards, of course, and backwards — back into your mouth, into the spaces behind your nose and down your throat! If you play a reasonably strong low note, you might even be able to *feel* it in your throat, *if* your mouth and throat are unconstricted as when you yawn. Try it.

Now it is also a fact that, in order to add volume and body to their sound, most instruments incorporate a 'resonator' of some kind, very often simply a contained space in which the sound can 'echo'; violins, cellos and guitars have hollow wooden bodies; xylophones have empty tubes or boxes under their keys. **You** have those spaces inside you where the sound of your flute can circulate. The lowest notes of your range in particular need all the help they can get, so — always maintain an open throat and, so far as possible, keep your tongue low and out of the way so that the sound can circulate and echo and, finally, come shooting out again, new and enriched.

Your 'cavities' will not only boost the volume of your flute (a little) but, depending on how you shape them, they will also colour its tone. Your mouth is most important here. As you play a note, try 'mouthing' different vowels — 'ee', 'e', 'eu', 'oo', and 'eye', for instance. I like 'eu' because it has both edge and fullness. See which you prefer.

Lastly, don't muffle the flute. For the low notes, keep your top lip over your bottom lip and your bottom jaw pushed out. Also, leave plenty of the blow-hole open; only cover between a quarter and a third.

If all this has no effect, jump forward to page 56. What you read there may be more immediately helpful.

For reference, here are the fingerings for the two lowest notes on your flute:

BOTTOM C♯/D♭   BOTTOM C

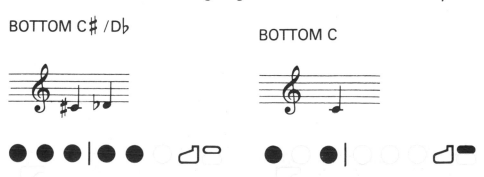

Dotted half-notes

A note with a dot placed after it should last for its own written time plus half as much again.

In $\frac{4}{4}$ time, this: 𝅗𝅥 lasts for two beats.

Half of two is one, so this: 𝅗𝅥. lasts for three beats. (2 + 1)

Dotting a note is a shorthand way of writing a common combination of tied notes; 𝅗𝅥. will sound just the same as 𝅗𝅥 𝅘𝅥, which is something that you have already played.

A dotted half-note can only appear in two places in a $\frac{4}{4}$ bar and should be counted like this:

THE OUTLANDISH KNIGHT contains some dotted half-notes and lots more low and high Ds for you to practise.

THE OUTLANDISH KNIGHT

ENGLISH TRAD.

A new time signature — $\frac{3}{4}$

Music having only 3 beats in a bar is just as common and easy to count as music with 4. A basic three-time rhythm goes like this:

```
Clap   steadily    *   *   *   *   *   *   *   *   *
       Count        1   2   3   1   2   3   1   2   3
```

In $\frac{3}{4}$ time, ♩ represents 1 beat, as it did in $\frac{4}{4}$ time.

So, ♪ still lasts for 2 beats.

And ♩. still lasts for 3 — that's a whole bar, now.

𝅝 can't be used in $\frac{3}{4}$ (because one would be longer than a bar). The equivalent rest

can be used, though. ▬ means 'rest for a whole bar', and it can be used in this way

regardless of the time signature.

Clap each of the rhythms below over and over until you have the feel of them. Count out loud at first, and then silently, being careful not to leave a gap after each 3 for a silent 4.

```
    1    2    3      1   (2)   3      1    2   (3)      1   (2)   (3)
```

Here is the rhythm of a well-known Christmas carol. You will find the complete tune on page 55, along with some other tunes in $\frac{3}{4}$ time, but try to work out what it is before you turn the page.

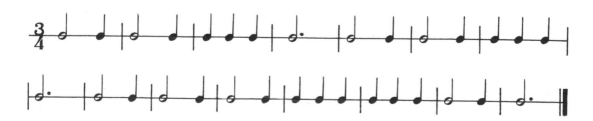

53

THE COVENTRY CAROL

MEDIEVAL DANCE

WE THREE KINGS

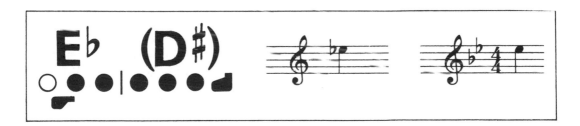

Notice that, except for the addition of the little finger, the fingerings for these two notes are just the same as the two D fingerings that you already know.

If E♭ appears in the key signature of a piece, it will be written in the top space of the stave and always accompanied by a B♭.

In **PLAISIR D'AMOUR**, D to E♭ to D is just a wiggle of the little finger.

PLAISIR D'AMOUR

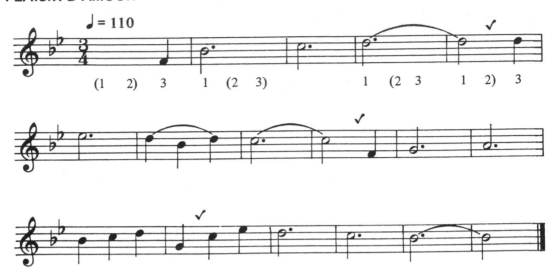

More tone improvement

If you reduce the size of your lip opening, the air which passes through it will be concentrated — more air will be aimed at one spot — and automatically accelerated. Your breath behaves like the water which only trickles out of your bath tap until you partly block the outlet with your thumb or your toe; **then** the water comes out with real force. It's the same amount of water under the same pressure — the size of the opening controls the speed.

At this stage you may well find that concentrating and accelerating the air-jet has a beneficial effect on your tone. Assuming that you are already blowing in a positive manner, there should be no need to blow harder (or put your toe in your mouth!) to achieve this; just flatten the air-jet by bringing your top lip closer to your bottom lip. Attempt to make your air-jet narrower only if it is already wider than the blow-hole.

As you flatten the air-jet you may find that you need to aim it a little more delicately, and you may need to re-centre the flute slightly, but as a result, the tone should harden and brighten.

When you are successful in producing this shinier tone, listen very carefully to yourself, and try this;

1) Play a G with a rather open embouchure so that the tone is windy and dry.
2) Slowly tighten the embouchure to get the brighter sound described above. Notice that the dull tone doesn't in fact 'turn into' the brighter tone but remains as a sort of background; the new sound is apparently separate and fades in over the top. The effect is curiously three-dimensional. **Balancing** these two sounds can give richness, depth and edge to your tone.

Don't worry if what I have described takes some time to achieve. These two exercises should help you gain the control you need.

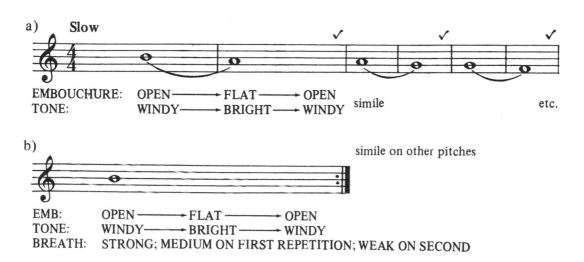

Eighth-notes or Quavers

An eighth-note lasts for half the time of a quarter-note, so in $\frac{3}{4}$ and $\frac{4}{4}$ times, it will last for half a beat.

One eighth-note looks like this: ♪

But for the moment you will only see them in pairs, in which case they are joined together like this:

The first eighth-note of a pair is played on the beat — with the count. The second starts exactly half way through the beat — *between* counts. Four beats of eighth-notes are counted like this:

1   and   2   and   3   and   4   and

It is very important that the eighth-notes of each pair are the same length so that the beat is evenly divided. To get the feel of this, clap a quickish but comfortable pulse and count against it as follows:

Clap   *   *   *   *   *   *   *   * | *   *   *   *   *   *   *   *
Count   1   &   2   &   3   &   4   & | 1   2   3   4

In normal notation that would be written:

Try the rhythms below:

Now clap the rhythms that you counted, instead of the eighth-note pulse.
Try to think of '1 &', '2 &' etc. as single two-syllable words to be said on the beat.

HAJEJ, NYNEJ

CZECH FOLK SONG

1   2   +   3   (4)

i   2   +   3   4   +

SIMPLE GIFTS

AMERICAN TRAD.

Read page 47 again to check on the best way to deal with tied rhythms in THE TROUT.

You will find a piano accompaniment for the next piece in the supplement.

THE TROUT

SCHUBERT

BAMBOO FLUTE is in $\frac{2}{4}$ time — just two beats (quarter-notes) in a bar.

HSIAO — BAMBOO FLUTE

CHINESE TRAD.

C♯ is not so much fingered as unfingered, so it presents the ultimate test of your grip.

On almost all flutes, this C♯ sounds a bit too sharp and has a weak tone. You will need to compensate for this by hardening the tone a little and pushing the lips forward.

Leaving the second and third fingers of the right hand down can actually help the tone and tuning of this note, but can create a fingering problem. In a quick change from D to C♯ and back, however, leaving one or both of those fingers down instead of your little finger *can* make the fingering easier.

Like this:

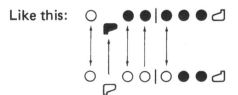

*A♯ is the same note as B♭ . Be sure to use this fingering;

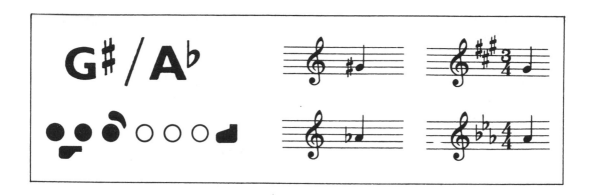

This note fits between G and A. Its two names are used with equal frequency.

You need your left little finger to play this note, so if you have been tucking it away, now is the time to bring it out. Always keep it poised and ready for use over the G♯ key from now on.

Practise **THE KEYS OF CANTERBURY** slowly. When you have mastered any fingering problems that there may be, take it more and more quickly until it becomes a jig.

THE KEYS OF CANTERBURY   **ENGLISH TRAD.**

Don't be frightened off by the length of this tune; much of it is simple repetition. It contains all five sharps, by the way — three in the key signature (F#, C# and G#) and A# and D# as accidentals.

RUTH'S TUNE

A Recap on Tone Quality

You have now played all the notes in the 'lower register'. A set of higher notes will be introduced shortly and you will manage them more effectively and with greater ease if you have done everything you can to strengthen and clarify the tone of the notes that you already know. So far as going on to the second register is concerned, strengthening the notes from A up to E♭ is most important. Perhaps this summary of the factors which affect the tone of your flute will help you do this:

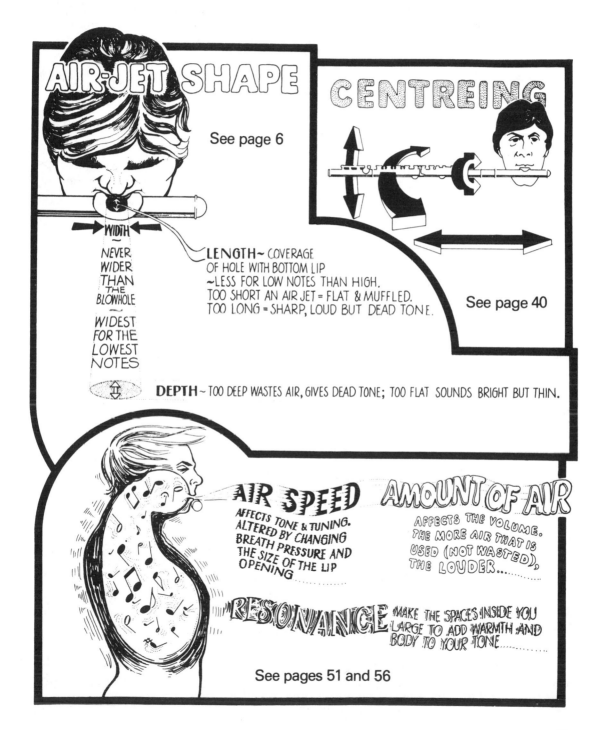

AIR-JET SHAPE

See page 6

WIDTH

NEVER WIDER THAN THE BLOWHOLE ~ WIDEST FOR THE LOWEST NOTES

LENGTH~ COVERAGE OF HOLE WITH BOTTOM LIP ~LESS FOR LOW NOTES THAN HIGH. TOO SHORT AN AIR JET = FLAT & MUFFLED. TOO LONG = SHARP, LOUD BUT DEAD TONE.

CENTREING

See page 40

DEPTH~ TOO DEEP WASTES AIR, GIVES DEAD TONE; TOO FLAT SOUNDS BRIGHT BUT THIN.

AIR SPEED
AFFECTS TONE & TUNING. ALTERED BY CHANGING BREATH PRESSURE AND THE SIZE OF THE LIP OPENING

AMOUNT OF AIR
AFFECTS THE VOLUME. THE MORE AIR THAT IS USED (NOT WASTED), THE LOUDER.........

RESONANCE
MAKE THE SPACES INSIDE YOU LARGE TO ADD WARMTH AND BODY TO YOUR TONE.........

See pages 51 and 56

The Second Register

In order to play all the notes for almost an octave above the notes that you now know, it won't be necessary to learn any new fingerings at all, only a new way of blowing the old ones. This is because each of the lower register fingerings from E upwards will produce a note an octave higher than the one that you are used to, if you

(a)   speed up the air in the air-jet, chiefly by reducing the size of the lip opening (you have already practised this, page 56), AND

(b)   shorten the gap between the lip opening and the blow-hole edge.

Shortening the opening-to-edge gap involves pressing the centre portions of both lips forwards, and will only be possible if you are supporting your bottom lip properly, leaving it free to 'unroll'. The action is something like saying 'EEEE-OOOO' except that you shouldn't allow the ends of your lips to be drawn in.

As you shift the centres of your lips forwards and tighten the embouchure to reduce the size of the lip opening, it will also be necessary to draw the bottom jaw in a fraction to correct the angle of the air-jet; now that the jet is shorter, it will need to be pointed down a little if it is still to split evenly on the edge.

Try using this movement to get you from a low E to E an octave higher. There is no need to change the fingering.

Throughout the entire range of the flute, if all the notes are to sound in the right octave and with the best possible tone, **all** the following transitions will need to be made smoothly:

	Low notes ←——→ High notes	
Lip opening	large _____	small
Speed of the air	slow _____	fast
Opening-to-edge distance.	long_____	short
Air-jet angle	⭢ _____	⭢

As you can see, a shift of a tone or so will only call for tiny adjustments to the embouchure, but the alterations needed to effect an octave leap will be quite noticeable and will have to be executed quite deliberately.

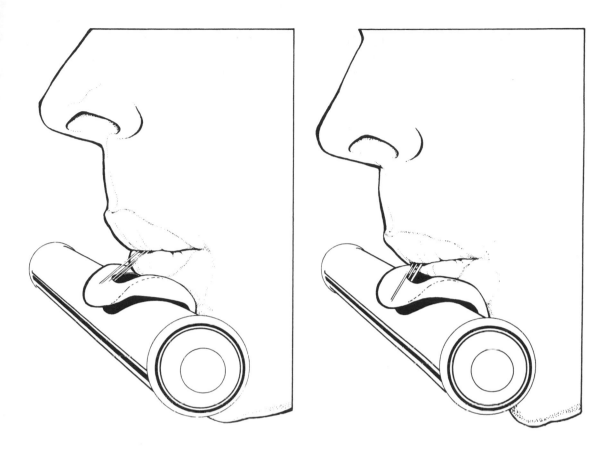

Blowing a low-ish note. . . . . and a **very** high note

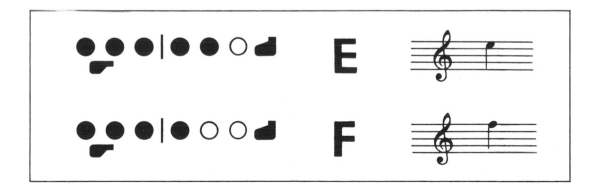

If you managed to play E, F should be no problem. Approach it in two ways — 1) from D, through E♭ and E, and 2) by leaping up from the F below, using just the same lip movements that you used to get you up to E.

Blowing E and F should be very little different from blowing D and Eb **if** you play them with a strong, clear tone. If you find that leaping to the E and F produces something rather better than your normal D/Eb—sound, try the new embouchure on those notes too.

RUSSIAN TUNE (CANON)

QUEM PASTORES only goes up to E, but will give you a chance to practise the awkward C — D — E change legato. Don't forget to put your right little finger down for E.

QUEM PASTORES

MINUET

Dotted Quarter-Notes

A dotted note lasts for its own written time plus half as much again, so where a quarter-note lasts for one beat, a dotted one will last for one and a half.

This means that a dotted quarter-note is the shorthand equivalent of a quarter-note and an eighth-note tied together, and *that* is something that you have already played — in **THE TROUT**, for instance.

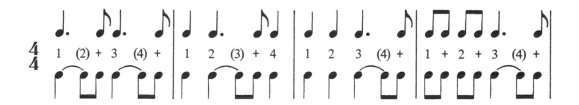

Master these rhythms before you go on to the pieces. They are written out with their tied versions underneath.

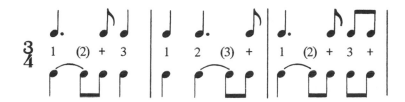

GREENSLEEVES

The second half of **GODDESSES** is tricky, but worth the effort it requires.

GODDESSES and VARIATION

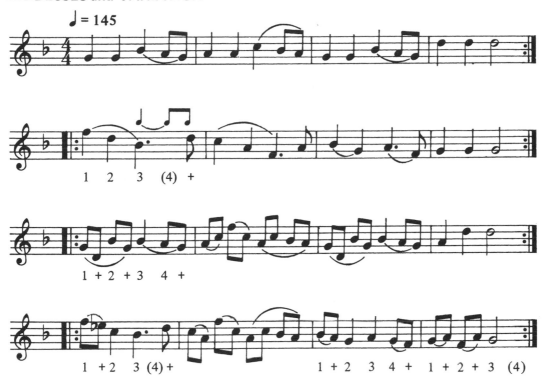

STOLEN RAGS

71

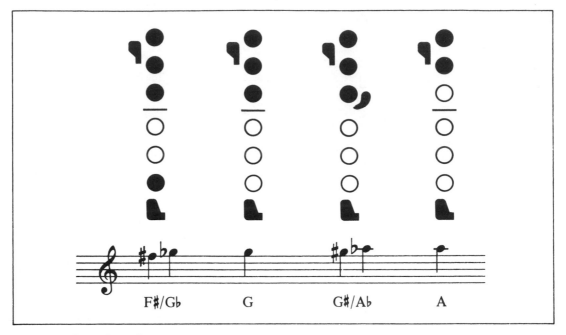

| F♯/G♭ | G | G♯/A♭ | A |

No new fingerings here.

If you find these notes difficult, look at the section on 'Harmonics' (page 74). Also, try this: play a note that you find easy to play, say D, with as strong and full a tone as you can muster. Then move higher and higher — D♯ —E—F—F♯ —G—G♯ —A, adjusting your embouchure as you go. Unless you are satisfied with the strength and clarity of one note, don't move on to the next. If the tone begins to deteriorate, rest and then go back a couple of steps. If you get a horrible grinding noise when you play these notes, it is probably because your lip opening is too large and/or too far from the blow-hole edge.

THEME FROM "SWAN LAKE"
TCHAIKOVSKY

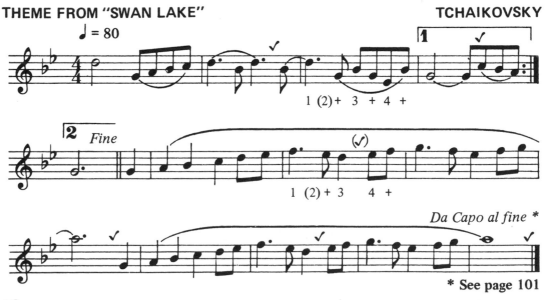

* See page 101

L'HOMME ARME

Before you play ORIGINAL RAGS, look at page 47 again for some advice on how best to handle tied rhythms.

ORIGINAL RAGS

SCOTT JOPLIN

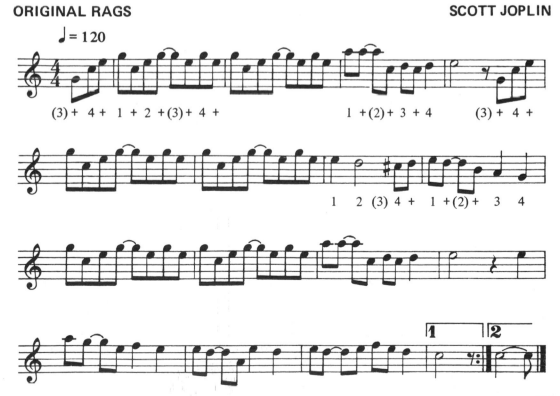

SCARBOROUGH FAIR

TRAD. MELODY

Harmonics

You have already discovered that bottom-register fingerings will each give you two notes, depending on the way that you blow them. In fact, they will give you more. A low D fingering, for instance, will yield not only a low D, but also the D which you normally play with your first finger raised, the A which is written above the stave, another D above that, then an F♯ and an A. Notes played with the 'wrong' fingering in this way are called harmonics.

Although you might find the higher ones difficult at this stage, the first and second harmonics of your lowest notes should be possible, and there is a very good reason for playing them. Standard fingerings are fairly tolerant — an approximate style of blowing will generally yield some sort of noise at the right pitch. Harmonic fingerings are much less tolerant. For instance, the A written above the stave **can** be played with a bottom D fingering, but it simply won't appear unless your embouchure is just right. This means that harmonics are a wonderful guide; if you can play a note as a harmonic so that it sounds reasonably secure and strong, then you can be sure that you have come very close to finding the best way of producing the same note with its standard fingering.

So — play as strong and clear a bottom D as you can.

Don't change the fingering — use the lip movement described on page 66 to make that D jump up an octave. Remember — don't move the flute, don't move your head, don't change the fingering and don't blow harder (a *little* extra breath pressure is all right) — make the leap by contracting the lip opening, pushing it forward and angling the air-jet down a fraction.

Keep this motion going — smaller gap, further forward, down more — and, with a little searching and experimentation perhaps, you should find yourself playing an A.

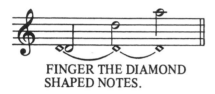

FINGER THE DIAMOND
SHAPED NOTES.

You *might* find yourself playing higher notes. Don't fight them, but search out the A (compare it with your normally fingered or low A to be sure).

If the A sounds bright and secure, switch smartly to your standard A fingering without altering the way that you are blowing at all. (You might like to leave your F♯ finger down to stop the flute from jerking.) You should now have a good A.

If this doesn't work, do try again. If it does — when it does — make a mental note of your embouchure, if and how it differs from your normal one. Also, practise going DDADD etc. all from the low D fingering and try the same thing starting on low C, C♯ and E. This will do wonders for your embouchure.

'Prepare' the first note of Erik Satie's **3rd GYMNOPEDIE** as a harmonic. You will find a piano accompaniment for this piece in the supplement. The '4' over the first bar of this piece and the special form of rest underneath it indicate that you should rest for four full bars when the pianist starts playing. Then you begin.

GYMNOPEDIE No 3

ERIK SATIE

†/** see page 101

Staccato

You have seen how a dot after a note affects its length. A dot placed *under* or *over* a note, like this:

tells you to sound only the first half of the note, leaving the other half silent. Writing this effect out in full is clumsy and fussy and involves lots of rests:

Staccato notes should generally be tongued, but resist the temptation to stop them with your tongue. This gives a hard ending to the note — this sort of shape:

A lighter, more relaxed effect can be achieved by using a separate bullet of air for each note. This is the panting like a dog that I mentioned in the breathing exercise at the start of the book, except that inhaling between each little jab is not necessary, even though it might help you to get the effect right at first. By this method, notes should have a clean start and a natural, resonant ending, like this:

To get this right, practise the staccato passages in the next piece without using your tongue at all. Aim for a clean start to each note — no coughing to get them going — and make the lips firmer than usual because otherwise all these jabs of air will distort your embouchure and spoil your tone. When you are reasonably satisfied, bring in your tongue, but merely to enhance the start of the note. By the way: there is no need to be too literal about playing staccato notes half length. For the moment, aim to make them simply detached, but with a clean, full tone.

RONDEAU

J. S. BACH

Dynamics

There are a number of signs and terms which tell you how loudly or quietly you should play a piece or a part of a piece. They are called 'dynamic markings' and from quietest to loudest, they are:

pp — short for *pianissimo*, Italian for 'very quiet'
p — *piano* — quiet.
mp — *mezzo-piano* — moderately quiet.
mf — *mezzo-forte* — moderately loud.
f — *forte* — loud.
ff — *fortissimo* — very loud.

crescendo (*cresc.* for short) means 'get *louder* gradually'.
diminuendo (*dim.*) means 'get *quieter* gradually'.

The last two effects can also be asked for with 'hairpins' —

getting louder   getting quieter

Playing loudly or quietly is not simply a question of how hard you blow.

When playing loudly:
1) Breathe deeply — blow through a relaxed, open throat — don't tense up — make a conscious contraction of the stomach and chest to expel the air.
2) Relax the embouchure a little — a slightly larger than normal lip opening will be necessary to allow an ample supply of air to the flute.
3) Make any embouchure adjustments that may be necessary to counter any sharpness or loss of clarity. (Don't let it sound like a fog-horn.)

When playing quietly:
1) Breathe deeply — open throat — now the stomach and chest should be in a state of tension. Particularly for high, very quiet notes, feel that someone is about to hit you in the stomach and brace yourself accordingly.
2) Make the lip-opening a little smaller to limit the supply of air, but not so much that the tone becomes thin and mean.
3) Adjust the embouchure to counter flatness and dullness.

Here are two invaluable exercises. Practise them on notes from throughout your range. Aim for a full tone and good, steady tuning.

i)   SLOW — a full breath for each note.

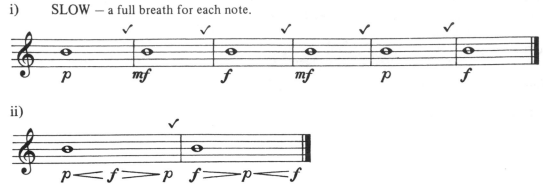

Now try this:

"SPRING", FROM "THE FOUR SEASONS"   **VIVALDI**

Sixteenth-Notes or Semiquavers

The sixteenth-note, or semiquaver, is the last and smallest time-value that you will meet in this book, although there are others.

One on its own looks like this ♪

Groups of two or more can be joined together in the same way that eighth-notes are:

In $\frac{2}{4}$, $\frac{3}{4}$ and $\frac{4}{4}$ times, a sixteenth-note lasts for a quarter of a beat. Groups of four

(a beat's-worth) should be counted like this:

1   an   &   a   2   an   &   a   3   an   &   a   etc. (**One**-an'-and-a **Two**-an'-and-a **Three**-an'-and-a)

To get the feel of how sixteenth-notes fit with quarter and eighth notes, clap a quick, comfortable pulse and count against it as follows:

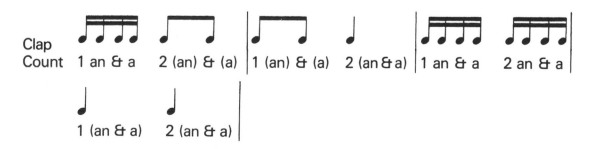

When you've got it, just mouth the counting, then just think it. Now you know how the rhythm of the next piece goes!

DANCE OF THE MIRLITONS

TCHAIKOVSKY

ARKANSAW TRAVELLER

The next piece should be gentle and spacious. Play it in a room, or hall, with plenty of echo.

BEACON PLAIN

* ⌢ is a fermata. You can hold a note with one of these for longer than written *ad lib.*

Sixteenth and eighth-notes can be mixed within the same beat, but only in five different ways. Practise each possibility again and again until you have the feel of it. Then try combining two or three of the patterns, one after the other.

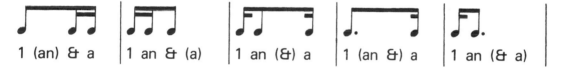

Notice the dotted eighth-notes. A straight eighth-note is worth two sixteenth-notes so a dotted one is worth three.

CAPRICE THEME

PAGANINI

♪. ♪ needn't be snappy and quick, of course; in the **'NEW WORLD'** it is very smooth.

THEME FROM "THE NEW WORLD SYMPHONY"　　　　　　　　DVORAK

THEME FROM SYMPHONY No 7　　　　　　　　BEETHOVEN

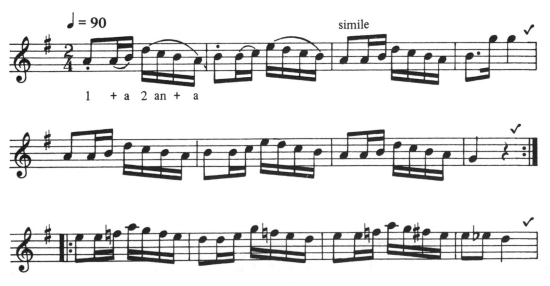

$\frac{3}{8}$ Time

In $\frac{3}{8}$ time there are three beats in a bar — 123 123 123 — just as there are in $\frac{3}{4}$ time, but in $\frac{3}{8}$ an eighth-note rather than a quarter-note is used to indicate one beat. In other words $\frac{3}{8}$ doesn't sound or feel different from $\frac{3}{4}$, it's just a different and sometimes more convenient way of writing the same thing. Read page 17 again if this mystifies you.

In $\frac{3}{8}$ ♪ = 1 beat, so ♩ = 2 beats and ♩. = 3 beats. ♪ = a ½ beat

You already have the feel of three-time rhythms so you will quickly get used to these new values. Here are some rhythms to clap and count, written in $\frac{3}{8}$ and $\frac{3}{4}$ for comparison.

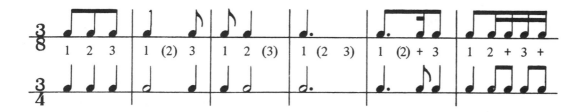

PRESTO **DEVIENNE**

HOBOECKENTANZ(!) **SUSATO**

EL VITO VITO

SPANISH TRAD.

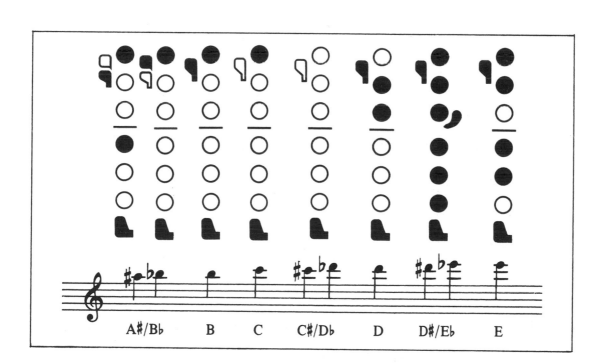

A♯/B♭	B	C	C♯/D♭	D	D♯/E♭	E

Look carefully at the fingerings for high D, E♭ and E. They are **new**.

Some more work with harmonics will help you to find just the best way of blowing these notes. First of all, repeat the exercise from page 75 over and over, each time a semitone higher. Remember that you shouldn't need to blow particularly hard or move the flute or your head. It is the lips and jaw that move.

Then try this:

Finally, here is a tune to be played entirely on harmonics. Make it as quiet, smooth and mysterious as the desert it came from.

AL YA ZANE   **TRAD. SYRIAN**

Your embouchure should now be well prepared to play all these high notes with their standard fingerings.

Any of the tunes from the start of this book (pages 30 to 64) will provide good practice-material if you simply play them an octave higher than they are written (a high A instead of a low one and so on).

Look again at page 47 for the best way to deal with tied rhythms before you play
ELITE SYNCOPATIONS. You will find a piano accompaniment for this piece in the
supplement.

ELITE SYNCOPATIONS   *SCOTT JOPLIN*

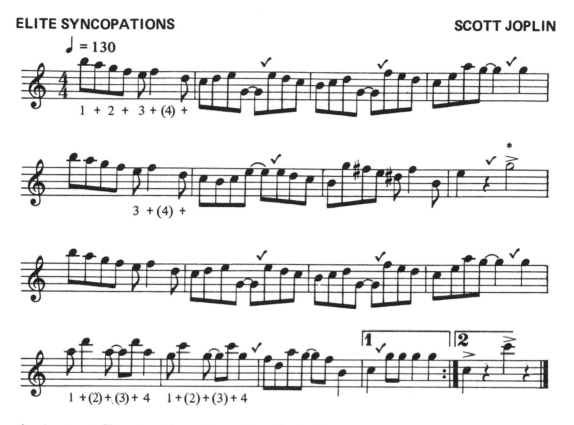

* > is an accent. Play notes with accents over them with extra force.

Why not write in your own phrasing for this Bach **MINUET**?

MINUET FROM "THE ANNA MAGDALENA NOTE BOOK"

J. S. BACH

1st PLAYER

2nd PLAYER

90

$\frac{6}{8}$ Time

In $\frac{6}{8}$ time there are six beats to a bar, and one beat is written as an eighth-note. The six beats are grouped and accented like this:

The feeling here should be of two strong beats in a bar (the first one stronger) with each beat divided into three, so it is better to count them like this:

Of course, apart from the <u>1</u> needing to be stronger than the <u>2</u>, a bar of $\frac{6}{8}$ is just like two bars of $\frac{3}{8}$ stuck together and you will find it easier to read if you think of it in this way. In the piece below, each bar has been divided into two $\frac{3}{8}$ bars for you. In other pieces you might find it useful to do the same for yourself.

THE FINE COMPANION

ENGLISH TRAD.

DRIVE THE COLD WINTER AWAY

ENGLISH TRAD.

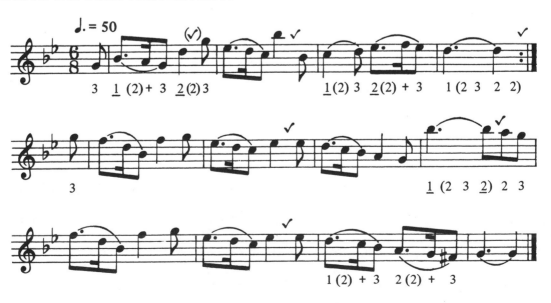

PART THREE
Going on

I hope that this book has worked for you and that you want to develop your new art further. In these last few pages you will find some information which should help you to do that. You will also find piano accompaniments for three of the pieces from earlier on in the book, guitar accompaniments for almost all of the others, and some general information which should prove useful.

Where to go from here

How do you progress from here? The most important thing is simply to play regularly, exploring as much music as possible. Playing with other musicians makes this more fun and will improve your musicianship very quickly, so join or form some sort of group, orchestra or ensemble if you can. Listen to, and observe other players closely. Listen to yourself closely, too — on tape, if possible. Non-studio recordings are rarely flattering, so if you can make your playing acceptable on tape, you can be sure that you sound fine when you are 'live'.

If you aren't already having lessons, you may find that a good teacher can be a tremendous help. Lessons can be expensive, so don't agree to them without meeting and knowing something about the teacher first. Look for someone whose approach interests you, and someone you feel you can get on with. Give the teacher a trial period — remember that **you** are the customer. If you can't afford regular lessons, ask for an occasional 'check-up'.

Most teachers will introduce you to scales, arpeggios and studies. What are they?

Most pieces of music use only a selection of the twelve available notes. If you arrange the notes used in a particular piece in ascending order, starting and ending on the 'tonic' — this is usually the note the tune finishes and *feels* finished on — you will then have a scale, a simple ladder of notes. There are various good reasons for practising running up and down the most common of the many possible scales. Probably the most obvious one is that a large proportion of any tune is likely to be made up of the same little stepwise runs which constitute scales. Practising a scale means that you can master many of the fingering problems that may arise in a piece (in *every* piece using the same scale) before you play it. Scales also give you a chance to practise different articulation patterns without the distraction of having to learn new notes, and, at the same time, the lip movements necessary to keep a good tone as you move from register to register.

Arpeggios are the patterns of two- and three-note jumps most commonly found in classical and folk music and are practised for just the same reasons. A book such as the 'Rubank Advanced Method for Flute' will take you through all of these.

A 'study' is a piece of music especially written to feature a particular technical problem — playing large leaps legato, for instance. Playing a study — simply getting through the notes — won't in itself improve your playing; it's really up to you to bring a problem-solving attitude to your playing of the study. There are lots of graded studies available, written to help you tackle your own problems in as pleasant a way as possible. If working with scales, arpeggios and studies suits your temperament, the kind of music you want to play and the way you want to play it, then go ahead.

Unfamiliar Rhythms

Sooner or later, you are going to come across rhythms that are more complex than you are used to, or unfamiliar time signatures.

The more complex rhythms might contain some of these: ♪ — 1/32 notes (demisemiquavers, believe it or not) or even some of these: ♫ — 1/64 notes (yes! — hemidemisemiquavers.)

If you come across groups of these notes, don't try to count them unless the tempo is very slow; try instead — this is easy to *say* — to see and hear the simple rhythm inside the complex one. For instance, regard this:

as a fancy version of this:

Practise the simple version first, then just 'decorate' it with the extra notes in the complex version. Don't expect complicated-looking music to *sound* complicated, by the way; the chances are that it will sound quite unsurprising.

For any rhythm that you just cannot fathom, remember that all rhythms can be notated in a number of ways, some of which will look less off-putting than others; so rewrite the music, by simply doubling the note values. For instance, the 'complex' phrase above 'doubled' becomes this:

'Double' it again and add some extra barlines to make it easier to read (where the beats used to start and end) and you get this:

Now it should be easy. Learn it like this, then fit it back into the piece at the right speed.

The only new time signatures that you are likely to come across are those with a 9 or 12 on the top. Count them in groups of three — for instance 1 2 3 2 2 3 3 2 3 4 2 3 for 12-time.

Lastly, you are certain to come across 'triplets'. A triplet is three notes spread *evenly* through the time that is normally occupied by two. The commonest kind of triplet is

written like this  and takes up the time of

Vibrato

You may have noticed that most professional players' notes waver in an attractive sort of way. These controlled fluctuations in volume and pitch are called *vibrato*.

There is considerable debate among flautists concerning how strong this wavering should be, how much it should be used and whether, in the music of certain periods, it is right or authentic to use it at all. Nevertheless, used tastefully, vibrato is a subtle and expressive tool which can also add a general warmth and relaxation to your sound.

I should warn you that most teachers, myself included, put off teaching vibrato until their students can produce fundamentally even notes which are also precisely in tune. If you feel ready, go ahead.

Vibrato should only be added to a basically level and lump-free sound. If you feel that you can play a long low B which qualifies, then play it like this:

If that is smooth, lump-free and symmetrical, and nothing to do with your throat, then play this:

then this:

and so on, getting quicker and quicker until you are playing three to four *controlled* swells per second.

Don't hurry this. Let it take weeks, if necessary.

The other way to produce vibrato is to use the coughing muscles in the throat. Cough — very lightly and rhythmically! — into the flute, three or four times per second, maintaining a steady supply of air from the diaphragm. You should be producing separate, semi-staccato notes. Now gradually relax the coughing until it is inaudible — keep pushing the air out — and the separate notes join up.

Whichever technique you use (you should learn to do both) learn to control the speed **and** the depth of your vibrato. A shallow vibrato, at about four pulses a second, is probably the most generally usable.

Some special effects

Over the past 30 years or so, flautists have been discovering that their instrument has capabilities which had not previously been exploited in western music. They have discovered, for instance, that it is possible to play a number of notes on the flute simultaneously. These chords are called multiphonics. Every fingering will yield a multiphonic if you find just the right way to blow it, but the special fingerings below are relatively easy.

Blow the first three very gently, using a deep lip aperture. If you blow too hard you will lose the bottom note; too little breath will lose you the top note. Four and five should be played more loudly. Play the top note, then the bottom note, then move the lips back towards the top note position. Again, use a deeper than usual lip aperture. Both notes should appear when you are blowing 'between' the notes. Play six with a flat, compressed air-jet and high breath pressure. It is quite difficult, but worth it — it should sound alarmingly un-flute-like.

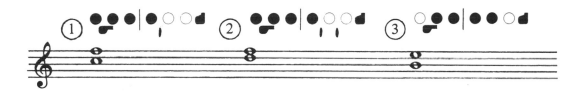

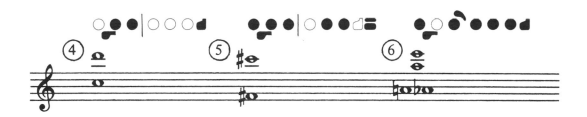

WHISTLE TONES are produced by fingering a note — bottom C is best — and then blowing a focused air stream very, *very* gently on to the blow-hole edge. You should hear quiet, high, distinct notes with a very delicate tone. As you increase your breath pressure, still higher notes will appear and by altering your breath pressure you can produce elaborate melodies from just the one fingering. If you have difficulties in finding these sounds, tilting the flute away from you might help.

Try to exclude the bottom C that you are fingering altogether, or, more subtle, see if you can make it fade in and out while the whistle tones continue above.

To really test and improve your breath control, try to latch on to one whistle tone and sustain it to the end of your breath!

By the way, if you've ever wondered how jazz and rock flautists like Ian Anderson produce that very rich, rough, buzzy sound, they do it by singing the same note that they are playing. For men, this usually involves singing falsetto.

If multiphonics, whistle tones and harmonics appeal to you, *Special Effects for the Flute* by Stokes and Condon (Trio Associates) will show you how to play them and various other so-called 'effects'. *Tone Development through Extended Techniques* by Robert Dick (Edu-Tainment) will show you ways of using these sounds to benefit your traditional playing.

Musical terms that you are likely to come across

a tempo — at the original speed
accelerando or *accel*. — gradually getting quicker
allegro — lively, quick
allegretto — a little less lively than allegro
andante — at a moderate speed, flowing
coda — a closing section for a piece, usually marked: Coda ⊕ ('to Coda ⊕' or 'al Coda'
        — jump from this point to the Coda.)
con — with
crescendo, cresc or ⟨⟨ — getting louder gradually
Da Capo, or *D.C.* — play again from the beginning
Da Capo al fine — play again from the beginning and as far as the word *'fine'*.
Dal Segno, or *D.S.* — play again from the sign: ꞷ.
Dal Segno al fine — play again from the sign ꞷ as far as the word *'fine'*.
diminuendo, dim — getting quieter gradually (also ⟩⟩)
dolce — sweetly
fine — the place to stop after the final repeat
forte — loud
largo — slow. spacious
legato — smoothly, linking the notes
lento — slowly
meno mosso — a little slower
mezzo-forte, mf — moderately loud
mezzo-piano, mp — moderately quiet
moderato — moderately
molto — very
pianissimo, pp — very quiet
piano, p — quiet
piu — more
poco — a little (poco piu mosso — a little more slowly)
poco a poco — little by little
presto — fast
rallentando, rall. — slowing down
ritardando, rit. — slowing down
sempre — always
senza — without
simile — carry on in the same manner
sforzando, sfz — a heavy, forced accent
staccato — detached
subito — suddenly
vivace — lively, vivacious

* Pronunciation guide: the stressed syllable is underlined.

Fingering Chart

This chart gives the fingerings for all the available notes on your flute. (That includes a whole octave that you haven't played yet.) The top four or five notes are difficult and rarely occur in pieces. See page 66 for the general principles behind playing the top register.

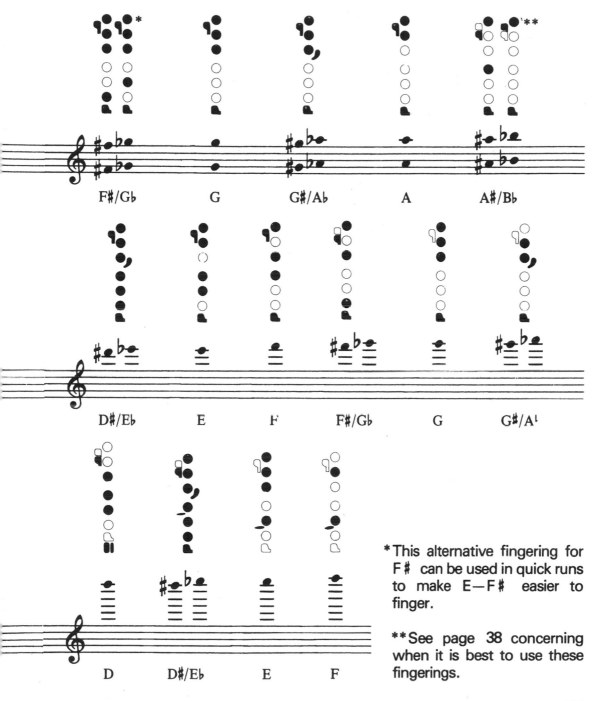

F#/Gb   G   G#/Ab   A   A#/Bb

D#/Eb   E   F   F#/Gb   G   G#/Al

D   D#/Eb   E   F

*This alternative fingering for F# can be used in quick runs to make E—F# easier to finger.

**See page 38 concerning when it is best to use these fingerings.

GUITAR ACCOMPANIMENTS

Page 34 **Streaked with jewels**

$\frac{4}{4}$ G B7 Em D7 | G F C B7 | E / / / | Am / / F | C / B7 / |‖1 Em / / / :‖2 Em ‖

Page 36 **Ilkerton Ridge** ♩ = 120

$\frac{4}{4}$ Dm/C | Dm/F | C | Em | Dm/F | F | C | G/C | Dm/C |

| Dm/F | C | Em | Dm/F | G | Am |1 G/A :‖2 C | C ‖

Page 39 **Ronde** ♩ = 130

$\frac{4}{4}$ ‖: Gm | Dm | C | F | Gm | Dm | C | F :‖ : F | F | Dm | Bb | F Bb | C Dm | C | F :‖

Page 39 **When the saints go marching in** ♩ = 120

$\frac{4}{4}$ F | F | F | F | F | F | F | C7 | C7 | F | F7 | Bb | Bb | C7 | C7 | F :‖

Page 42 **Well-sung song** ♩ = 110

$\frac{4}{4}$ G | G | Am | Eb° | Em | C | D | C :‖1 ‖2 C | D | D | D7 | D7 | G |

| D | D7 | Bm | Em | D7 | G | G | D7 | Eb° | Em Am | G D7 | G | G ‖

Page 43 **Incantation** ♩ = 140

$\frac{4}{4}$ Gm | D | F7 | Bb | Cm7 | D | D7 | Gm :‖ F | Bb | Cm | D | Cm7 | D | D7 | Gm ‖

Page 45 **Tete-a-tete** ♩ = 110

$\frac{4}{4}$ | F | C F | C | F | F | C F | C | F | Bb | C F | Bb | C F | F | C F | C | F ‖

Page 46 **We shall not be moved** ♩ = 140

$\frac{4}{4}$ | G | G | D | D | D7 | D7 | G | G/ D7 G7 | C | E° | G D7 | C C7 | G | D7 | G | G ‖

Page 46   **Theme from Beethoven's "Choral Fantasia"** ♩ = 120

$\frac{4}{4}$ |G |D7 |G |D7 G |G |D7 |G D7 |G |D7 |

|G |D7 G D7 G |D7 G7 |C G D G |D7 |G D7 |G   ‖

Page 48   **De los Alamos vengo** ♩ = 140

$\frac{4}{4}$ |F |F |C |F |F |F |C |F :‖ Bb |F |C |F |

|Bb |F |C |F |F |F |C |F |F |F |C |F ‖

Page 48   **The sun and the moon** ♩ = 140

$\frac{4}{4}$ Em C |G |G |B7 |B7 |C |B7 |Em :‖: Em |Am |D7 |G |Em |Am |B7 |Em :‖

Page 50   **Chorale melody** ♩ = 80

$\frac{4}{4}$ Am7 |F C Dm C |G / C E |Am Am Esus E |Am / / :‖ Am |G Em F G7 |

|F / C / |Dm A7 Dm / |A / / D7 |G / C G |D / G C |Dm7 C G / |C / / ‖

Page 52   **The outlandish knight** ♩ = 130

$\frac{4}{4}$ D7 |G |Am C |D D7 |G |Am C |D |G |Em |C |D |Am |C |D |D / / :‖

Page 54   **The Coventry carol** ♩ = 90

$\frac{3}{4}$ Gm / D |Gm / Eb |F / Gm |D / / |Gm F Bb |C D / |G / / |G / / :‖ Gm / / |

|Gm / Bb |F / Gm |Dm / Gm |F / C |D / / |Gm D Gm |C D / |G / / |G / / ‖

Page 55   **We three kings** ♩. = 60

$\frac{3}{4}$ Em |Em |B7 |Em |Em |Em |B7 |Em |Em |D |G |G |Am |C B7 |Em |D7 |

|G |G |C |G |G |G |C |G |Em |D |Am7 |D |Em |G |C |G ‖

Page 56   **Plaisir d'amour** ♩ = 110

$\frac{3}{4}$ |Bb |F7 |Bb |Bb |Eb |Bb |F7 |F7 |Eb |F7 |Bb |Eb |Bb |F7 |Bb |Bb ‖

Page 59   **Hajej, Nynej** ♩ = 90

4/4   F |G7 C|G7 C|Gm Dm|C F |F Gm |B♭ C |F B♭|G C |F |G7 C |G7 C |B♭ F |C F ‖

Page 60   **Simple gifts** ♩ = 120

4/4 |G Em |D7 G |D |Am7 D7|G Em |D G |Am7 D |G C G / |G |

|D   G |G Em7|Am7 D |G C G D |Em Bm |Am7 D7 |G C G / ‖

Page 60   **The trout** ♩ = 120

4/4 |B♭ |B♭ |F |F F7 |B♭ |B♭ |F C7 |F |F7 |B♭ |

|F |B♭ B♭7 |E♭ |B♭ |F7 |B♭ |E♭ |B♭ |F7 |B♭   :‖

Page 62   **Pastime with good company** ♩ = 140

4/4   Bm|Bm |F♯m |F♯m|D |A Bm|F♯7 |Bm|Bm |Bm|F♯m|F♯m|D |A Bm|F♯7 |Bm / / |D|

|G/Em/|Bm//D|G/Em/|Bm|F♯m|F♯m//|D|G/Em/|Bm//D|G/Em/|Bm|Em F♯7|Bm‖

Page 63   **The keys of Canterbury** ♩. = 100
(Capo on 1st fret, piano transpose up a semitone)

3/4 |Em |C |G |G |D |B7 |Em |Em :‖Em |Am |Em |Em |

|C |Am |Em |Em |Em |C |Am7 |B7 |Em |Em |Em |Em ‖

Page 68   **Quem pastores** ♩ = 108

3/4   G |G |C |D |G |Am |Em/ A7|D7 |G |D |Bm |Em |Am |G |C / D7 |G ‖

Page 70   **Greensleeves** ♩ = 120

3/4 |Gm |Gm |F |F |Gm |Gm |D |D |Gm |Gm |F |F |Gm |D |Gm |Gm |

|B♭ |B♭ |F |F |Gm |Gm |D |D |B♭ |B♭ |F |F |Gm |D |Gm |Gm ‖

Page 71   **Goddesses and variation** ♩ = 145

4/4   Gm |F |Gm |D :‖‖: B♭ |F |Gm Dm |C Gm :‖
                                                 (Play twice)

Page 72   **Stolen rags** ♩ = 110

                                                        ⌐1   ⌐2

4/4   F F♯° |C7 |F F♯° |C7 |A7 Dm|D7 Gm |B° |C7 :‖F C7 |F   ‖

Page 72 **Theme from "Swan Lake"** ♩ = 80

$\frac{4}{4}$ GmCm|Gm |Gm/E°Eb° |GmDm:‖Gm ‖F |Bb |Eb |D |F |Bb |Eb |Cm D7 ‖

[1] [2] *fine*

D.C. al fine

Page 73 **L'homme arme** ♩. = 60

$\frac{3}{4}$ G |C |G D / |G |G |G |G |C / |G D / |G |G / :‖ / |

|G |D |G |D |G |D |G A / |D / |G |A / Em |F A / |D |D ‖

fine *D.C. al fine*

Page 73 **Original rags** ♩ = 120

$\frac{4}{4}$ |C |C |F Fm|C |C |C |D7 |G7 |C |C |F Fm |E7 |A7 |Dm Fm |G7 |C :‖

Page 74 **Scarborough Fair** ♩ = 110

$\frac{3}{4}$ Am |C |G |Am |C |Am |D |Am |Am |C |C |G |F |G |Em |Am ‖

Page 82 **Arkansaw traveller** ♩ = 90

$\frac{2}{4}$ F Bb |C F |C F |Bb C |F Bb |C F |F Bb |C F :‖

Page 83 **Caprice theme** ♩ = 85

$\frac{2}{4}$ Gm |D |Gm |D :‖G |Cm |F |Bb |A° |Gm |Eb7 D |G ‖

Page 87 **El vito vito** ♩. = 60

$\frac{3}{8}$ A |A |A |Dm |Dm |A |B° |A |A |A |A |Dm |

|Dm |A |G7 |A ‖: A |A |A |A |Dm |G7 |C |A :‖

Da Capo

Page 90 **Elite syncopations** ♩ = 130

$\frac{4}{4}$ G7 |C |G7 |C |G7 G#°|Am |Em B7 |Em G7|G7 |C |G7 |C |F |C |G7 |C :‖

Page 92 **The fine companion** ♩. = 80

$\frac{6}{8}$ Em |D |Em Bm |Bm Em |D |B7 |Em B7 |Em :‖

‖: G D |G B7 |Em D |G D7 |G D |A B7 |C Bm7|C Em :‖

Page 92 **Drive the cold winter away** ♩.= 50

[1] [2]

$\frac{6}{8}$ |Gm |Eb Gm|Cm Eb|D7 :‖D7 F7|Bb |Cm Eb|Bb Dm|Eb Cm|Bb |Cm Eb|Gm D7|Gm‖

Con ped.

GYMNOPEDIE No. 3 — PIANO PART

ERIK SATIE

To Coda ⊕

D.%. al Coda

⊕ *CODA*

ELITE SYNCOPATIONS — PIANO PART

SCOTT JOPLIN